ACCEPT No Imitations

ACCEPT No Imitations

JAMES W. ANGELL

Abingdon Press
Nashville

ACCEPT NO IMITATIONS

Copyright © 1984 by Abingdon Press

All rights reserved.
No part of this book may be reproduced in any manner whatsoever without written permission of the publisher except brief quotations embodied in critical articles or reviews. For information address Abingdon Press, Nashville, Tennessee.

Library of Congress Cataloging in Publication Data

ANGELL, JAMES W.
  Accept no imitations.
  1. Apologetics—20th century. 2. Christian life—Presbyterian authors. I. Title.
  BT1102.A56   1984   239   83-21364

ISBN 0-687-00692-9

Scripture quotations unless otherwise noted are from the Revised Standard Version of the Bible, copyrighted 1946, 1952, 1971, © 1973, by the Division of Christian Education of the National Council of the Churches of Christ in the U.S.A., and used by permission.

Those noted KJV are from the King James Version.

The Bible text noted NKJV is from The New King James Bible. Copyright © 1979, 1980, 1982, Thomas Nelson, Inc., Publishers.

Scripture noted Phillips is from The New Testament in Modern English, copyright © J. B. Phillips, 1958, 1959, 1960, 1972.

Quotations noted NEB are from The New English Bible. © the Delegates of the Oxford University Press and the Syndics of the Cambridge University Press 1961, 1970. Reprinted by permission.

Those noted TEV (Today's English Version) are from the *Good News Bible*—Old Testament: Copyright © American Bible Society, 1976; New Testament: Copyright © American Bible Society 1966, 1971, 1976.

The excerpt on page 26 is from the "Letters" column in *Time* magazine. Copyright 1983 Time Inc. All rights reserved.

MANUFACTURED BY THE PARTHENON PRESS AT
NASHVILLE, TENNESSEE, UNITED STATES OF AMERICA

The lines by Maria Rilke on pages 27-28 are from *Letters to a Young Poet*. Used by permission of W. W. Norton & Company.

The quotation on pages 32-33 is used by permission. Copyright © 1973, 1974, 1976 by Judith Viorst. From *How Did I Get to Be 40 & Other Atrocities*, published by Simon & Schuster.

The personal letters on pages 38 and 126 are used by permission of the letter writers.

The comments on self-esteem on page 41 are based on material from Ann Landers' column, which is controlled by the Field Newspaper Syndicate.

The poem "These Are Hard Directives" on pages 42-43 is from *alive now!* July/August 1979, copyright 1979, by The Upper Room, used by permission of Jane A. Peterson.

The lines on page 57 are from the play *For the Time Being*. Copyright 1944. Renewed 1972 by W. H. Auden. From W. H. Auden's *Collected Poems*, edited by Edward Mendelson. Reprinted by permission of Random House, Inc.

The quotation on page 70 is copyright 1983 Christian Century Foundation. Reprinted by permission from the January 19, 1983, issue of *The Christian Century*.

The quotation on pages 94-95 by James W. Angell is from *Ages & Stages: Christian Adulthood, Study Book 1*. Copyright © 1981 by Graded Press. Used by permission.

Quotation on page 104 is used by permission of Theodore Loder.

The excerpt on page 105 is from the song "Different Is Beautiful." Copyright © 1974 by Richard K. Avery & Donald S. Marsh. Used by *special permission*.

The lines from Rudyard Kipling's poem "If" on page 113 are used by permission of The National Trust and Macmillan London Limited.

The poem "Peter Runs Toward the Empty Tomb" on pages 124-25 is from *alive now!* July/August 1979, copyright 1979, by The Upper Room, used by permission of Sue Spencer.

The prayer on page 126 is from *Are You Running With Me, Jesus?* by Malcolm Boyd. Copyright © 1965 by Malcolm Boyd. Reprinted by permission of Holt, Rinehart and Winston, Publishers.

The poem "He Whom a Dream Hath Possessed" on pages 134-35 is reprinted from *Jealous of Dead Leaves*, selected verse of Shaemas O'Sheel, by permission of Liveright Publishing Corporation. Copyright 1928 by Boni & Liveright, Inc. Copyright renewed 1956 by Annette K. O'Sheel.

For Captain Gilbert H. Richards
and other shipmates of the
U.S.S. Moffett (DL 362)

CONTENTS

Introduction / *9*
1. Don't Take Any Wooden Emeralds / *13*
2. Fortran and a Fragrance / *26*
3. An Educated Heart / *38*
4. Amadeus and the Gospel / *50*
5. Peace Yes, Freedom Yes / *61*
6. Singleness and Marriage—
    A Double Celebration / *72*
7. Love at Any Age / *82*
8. Life Is a Ten-Foot Wall / *96*
9. The Athletes and the Rules / *108*
10. Run for Your Life / *119*
11. Raised Arms and Scoreboard Lights / *128*
12. Nothing Dies That Is Remembered / *136*

INTRODUCTION

Cartagena in Colombia, South America, is a mellow, marvelous old city—one of the oldest in the hemisphere. Its greatest claim to fame is not its age or its fortress, overlooking its invisibly barricaded harbor, but its emeralds.

But one does not go shopping for emeralds without a wariness about worthless imitations. And, to be honest, Virginia and I didn't go shopping at all when our ship, the *Golden Odyssey*, stopped at Cartagena in the course of a recent wedding anniversary cruise. We thought the emeralds would cost too much money.

The emerald is a variation of beryl and is the diamond's chief competitor among precious stones. In the Book of Revelation it is called the fourth foundation of the city of Jerusalem.

The religion "market" is equally as treacherous as the precious stones market. Because it deals with the deepest things in life—with personal and timeless ones—the lure is strong. And the possibilities of being defrauded are great. Yet an overcaution or a strict skepticism may also wind up closing the door to God and life, leaving us alone and freezing in the dark, left with only our selves, our doubts, our questions.

To risk the risk of faith is like allowing ourselves to fall in love, dangerous but worth it!

In the pages that follow I try to define a belief structure that is worthy of modern minds and hearts, one that deals more with daring hope than dogmatic certainties. I am an advocate for a faith that is not suspicious of today's super-sciences, but also one that is doubtful of their ability to define life's meaning apart from trust in Something and Someone beyond ourselves.

I believe that it is possible to affirm both an open future and a God of sovereign, redeeming activity, but too often these seem to be treated as mutually exclusive. The new 1984 world of computers, microbiology, international economics, sperm banks, teleconferencing, bio-sensors, jazzercise, and space platforms is left dangling, without a bridge for thoughtful people to cross back and forth on between the Bible's commentary on justice, sin, and resurrection, and those tough moral decisions that keep banging on the door asking for someone to supply a morally intelligent answer.

The demagoguery represented by the Moral Majority is repulsive to many of us. But, on the other side of things, there is also a dearth of leadership that sets forth alternative routes out of the bogs of violence, family smashups, and pale dreams.

Those who encourage a religion of manipulation—using it to get what they want, improved health, improved personality or improved finances—keep the air waves humming and the book stores busy. On the other hand, those who speak and write about excellence of both mind and heart—what Studdert-Kennedy called the "Splendid Spirit," the Force that calls us out of self-preoccupation, fear, and greed into greatness of soul and readiness of service—have begun to sound as dated as the Peace Corps.

Though it sounds trite to say so, this is definitely a new time, a time of "high tech," cable networks, surrogate mothers, artificial intelligence, direct dial to any place in the world, computers, robots, million-dollar homes, interchangeable human parts, more than thirty-two thousand people who have already lived beyond one hundred years of age. The information explosion won't quit. Four-fifths of *all* knowledge has been gained in the last forty years. Every week holds a celebration of some kind. And, perhaps symbolically, "coke" now means cocaine almost as often as it does that famous drink we associate with hamburgers. The year 1984 is here on schedule.

Can we affirm this new future—the best of it, not its worst? Can we shape it into those transcendent purposes of God that outweigh in meaning our cultural experimentations and capacity to mess things up? Can we make friends with technology? Can we find the right creative balance between God's ownership and our own responsibility for determining the form of tomorrow—recognize the difference between green glass imitations and cosmic emeralds? The coincidence of the Olympic Games in the United States with George Orwell's *Nineteen Eighty-Four* and our concern with a revival of excellence generally make our investigation a timely one.

The Spirit of God is our best resource for any human season. If that fails, we still have the contingency suggested by the last lines of George Herbert's poem, "The Pulley": "If goodness lead him not, yet weariness/May toss him to My breast."

James W. Angell

Don't Take Any Wooden Emeralds

The International Anticounterfeit Coalition, meeting in San Francisco, was told that brand name counterfeiting has grown from practically nothing in the mid-1970s to $16 billion a year. "Now there are fakes in virtually every field—auto parts, Vaseline, computers, shaving lotion and prescription drugs—and a few years ago the problem barely existed," James L. Bikoff, president of the coalition, said at its annual meeting.

—AP press release

If you've ever visited tiny Balboa Island just off the Pacific coastline near Newport Beach, California, you know that all its streets are named for gems. They are Topaz, Diamond, Amethyst, Ruby, Sapphire, and Emerald.

Most of these are mentioned in the Bible. Ever since our Caribbean cruise visit to Cartagena, which defines itself as the emerald capital of the world, I have had a special curiosity about emeralds.

In the Old Testament emeralds are listed among the precious stones used to adorn the priestly garments of Aaron. Ezekiel mentions them among expensive wares traded between Judah and the men of Rhodes—along with embroidered work, fine linens, ebony, agate, horses, mules, coral, purple, silver, tin, ivory tusks, wheat, olives, early figs, honey, oil, balm, white wool, wine, and vessels of bronze. In the New Testament the description of the new

Accept No Imitations

Jerusalem includes emeralds as one of the jewels used to adorn the foundations of the new city wall.

In today's world the advice, "Don't take any wooden nickels," can also be said for emeralds. The aim of this book is to say, "Let us not accept any wooden *emeralds* or glass ones either." Let us not substitute for true faith something that is scam, flimflam, fraudulent, cruel, divisive, unworthy of our highest human possibilities.

Some substitutes are fine. Astroturf may be preferable to grass for all-weather football. And we have long since adapted to margarine in place of butter, and detergents in place of soap. We may decide hamburger helper is a bargain. But we still have a preference for real diamonds in place of man-made ones, for sunlight rather than fluorescent fixtures. Those who promote the BMW automobile have a slogan, "There Are No Substitutes for Legends." While that is the glowing sort of commercial propaganda we've gotten used to, there is still something inside of us that rebels at lookalikes or at the words *simulated, imitation,* or *artificial.* When we attend the theater we still want to see the main actor or actress instead of a stand-in.

Religion, on its face, sounds intrinsically good. "Whatever helps people" is fine we tend to say. "All roads that lead to God are good. It matters not what your faith may be. All are but branches of a tree." "It's a free country." In a world that knows too much of

Don't Take Any Wooden Emeralds

terror and trouble, someone says, "Let us pray," and it sounds like the right thing to do.

But none of this justifies a pious silence or unwillingness to speak against religions that pervert the human spirit, that maim, that produce neuroticism in their adherents, that pander to curiosity and fear, that engender hate and division, that become still one more piece and particular of a counterfeit world.

I don't know that I ever saw or handled any counterfeit money, but, like many other people who have reached their adulthood, I've had plenty of exposure to fraud and misrepresentation.

The only station wagon I ever owned I owned just one week. I bought it one afternoon at Roger Dean's Used Car Lot on East Main. It was a pretty color, red with wood (imitation) trim. The kids liked it, and I drove it up and down the neighboring streets a few times. And, yes, the engine roared to life on a quick twist of the starter key. But, on closer inspection at home, after the deal had been signed, I found out that it was a vehicle on its last legs. Fortunately, I was allowed to return it and get my money refunded. That experience made me slightly wiser.

Most of us have had some experiences in which we've been lied to, or done a little lying ourselves. We're all probably aware of the big business of manufacturing lookalikes—everything from Jordache jeans and Longine watches to amphetamines and cameras—that are often falsely and illegally

Accept No Imitations

labeled to attest to quality, but are really disguised and usually inferior merchandise.

Should we call in the bunco squad? Notify the Better Business Bureau? Consult our attorney? Or suffer in silence because we allowed ourselves to be had?

Caveat emptor means "let the buyer beware," and we do try to keep our guard up. But we often wind up allowing ourselves to be fooled anyway—taken for a ride.

Where, though, are our protections, if there are any, from phony exploitative religious "products" in a free and pluralistic society where one taste or truth obviously doesn't suit all?

Karl Marx believed that all religions were self-serving schemes used to seize or keep power, to manipulate through superstition, for some to get rich by. That position still has enough evidence to defend it to make those of us who identify ourselves with institutional religion sad and ashamed.

It is an old question, but time to ask it again, What are the hallmarks of worthwhile religion? What was the difference between the religion of Jesus and the Pharisees? How can we know the difference between the fraudulent and the Real McCoy? Between the Elmer Gantrys and the Mother Teresas? Between those who serve God, speak for God, call persons into God's service and will, and those who simply work the street to their own advantage, exhorting us to "use" faith rather than allowing it to use us?

Don't Take Any Wooden Emeralds

It's time to stand up to bad religion.

Maybe this whole business doesn't bother you as much as it does me, but I don't like it. I don't even like the word *religion,* though it has a superb meaning: "to fasten, or bind together," like ligaments that integrate the bone structure of the body.

Of course, there are those terrible religious crimes across the years, including the Spanish Inquisition in the 1500s, Jonestown in 1979, and Khomeini's theocracy in Iran.

Religious films are usually of poor, uninteresting quality.

And religious *people*—watch out! Here come snobbishness and substitutions galore. Here come trafficking in God and preying on the troubles of others. Here come the fundamentalists and the fatalists, frequently the most intolerant of us all.

Because I am a minister and a father of four, I am sometimes asked if any of my children are especially "religious." I know the meaning of the question and try to respond with honest courtesy. But the reply I most want to give (and sometimes do) is, "I hope not."

Yet I am hopelessly hooked on trying to discover, know, and obey in love, the God who gave me life, the One whose footsteps I continue to be aware of, who will not leave me alone, who, through the mysterious self-revelation we know as Jesus Christ, has transformed everything I think and all my thoughts about whom and what I want to become.

In Southern California we experience every kind

of religious quackery imaginable. An organization named the "Church of Naturalism" becomes the locale of two midnight murders and turns out to be a front for a narcotics ring.

In Berkeley, the Spiritual Counterfeits Project is a ministry devoted to giving people greater awareness of the dangers of proliferating cultic movements.

In another part of the country an entire small town gets itself mail-order ordained to take advantage of clergy benefits on the tax form (note the term: "clergy benefits").

Ron Hubbard's Scientology Centers offer courses of "study" at $5.00 each. Hal Lindsey's *Late Great Planet Earth* with its theology of doom sells fifteen million copies. Robert H. Schuller stages an Easter pageant with tickets at $7.50 each.

Television turns into a gigantic religious ripoff, a modern snake-oil business—a billion-dollar bazaar offering books, trinkets, and intercessory prayers at bargain prices. Religion becomes a quick route to a Cadillac. And the more afraid people become of life, of their neighbors, and of the future, the bigger the scam becomes. God is for sale, and it's time someone blew the whistle.

Russell Chandler wrote in the *Los Angeles Times*, November 25, 1982:

> With the development of sophisticated computer technology, specialized donor lists that sell for $100 or more per 1,000 names and high-speed printing and mailing tech-

Don't Take Any Wooden Emeralds

niques, a new breed of direct-mail consultants has sprung up to service the religious market.

Not *all* religion is manipulation and exploitation. Some hold the candle of hope. Some deal with the most precious things on earth. Some address depths in humankind, huge blocs the rest of the human enterprise ignores. That's what makes its misuse tragic.

What *is* authentic religion? (For an answer, try Ecclesiastes 12:13 or James 1:27.) What does God ask, promise, or want from us? What challenges make their appeal on the *right* grounds, call out for greatness of life and daring of soul, rather than pandering and promising to meet all our needs, which could be one of the worst possible things God did to or for us.

What form of worship and devotion, if any, warrants our full loyalty? Which, if any, deserves our trust? Which has power to tell us who we are and what life is for?

Since courage, love, hope, and sacrifice are part of an invisible order of things, deceit is easy and certainty is impossible.

And there are but two options.

One, we can say an agnostic no to *all* religious risk. Risk nothing, except the death of indecision which has been called "shivering on the bank."

Or, we can take the leap of an unverified faith, dare with our hearts to trust God. We can read the Bible with discerning love, not as a bundle of proof texts and predictions, but as the drama of God's coming to care and to save.

We can "test the spirits," as John puts it (I John 4:1). We can search out the commitment offer that promises to give our lives meaning, that stakes a claim upon our brain, upon our love and possessions and that brings dignity, hope, and significance winging their way into both our inner and outer worlds.

There's nothing new, of course, about forgery. That's when we wind up with something less than the real—a copied signature, a reproduced Picasso, a twenty-dollar bill run off in a basement, or a zircon posing as a diamond. We wind up stuck with something that glistens but isn't gold. Fooled, framed, cheated. The Hitler diaries. The worthless mining stock.

This happens in the world of ideas and faith, too. I'm convinced we shouldn't settle for anything less or other than what life has power to ask of us or what God has given us power to become.

Let's not accept any wooden emeralds. There's too much good stuff around for that.

The good stuff is honest belief in an honest God. It is self-esteem based on a noble view of what it means to be human. It is faith in love—love that is not self-serving but extravagantly outreaching. It is a life of generous maximums, not legal minimums. It is belief that freedom is not so much automatic birthright as it is a fragile, superlative, expensive achievement.

The good stuff doesn't come in a bottle or between the pages of a book. It is hammered out on tougher altars.

A glassblower cannot create without a forge, and we cannot develop grown-up faith without having our faith and values tested in the laboratories of daily experience, in the serious cross-examinations of time. True Christian faith is made for Boston distances, has dimensions as wide as life itself. It urges us in the direction of personal sacrifice, rather than promised comfort. It shines with the mellow grace of a Cartagena at sunset. It offers all because it asks all. The inner earth pressure that produced the permanent jewelry of the ages has its correlative in another form of pressure: the *lure* of God.

Here are some characteristics which, for me, *disqualify* a faith as authentic.

First, it won't be worthy of our adherence if it is based on fear, or so preoccupied with the end of the world that the present winds up unaddressed. It won't be genuine if it is dishonest about difficulties, promising a life without them. Jesus' challenge "Are you able to drink the cup I drink of?" is a far cry from today's goal for success, happiness, health, a better body, or a larger income.

Second, since Jesus came to draw people together, not to divide them into cliques, it will also say no to religion that is exclusive instead of inclusive. Any church that warrants our celebration and loyalty will be one that expresses the risen presence of Christ, that represents a wide and interesting fellowship of all kinds of people, that is not a smug, self-righteous and separate sect.

A news item from the Los Angeles Times states:

> The Rev. William P. Gale of Mariposa, CA, in a broadcast sermon on national identity said: "If the Jews ever fool around with us or try to harm us in any way, every rabbi in L.A. will die within 24 hours."

Third, a faith that lacks a sense of the transcendent also lacks hope for a reconciled human community. A faith rich in the quality of hope will, on the other hand, accept responsibility for what we are becoming and how we can use God's gifts of time and reason. The Christian faith at its best travels among the stars.

And finally, we can never be really at peace with any interpretation of life that treats war as inevitable, or death as final. The future may be—is—dangerous but it is also radiant with possibility because God is part of it.

That's quite a necklace of negatives. But open the velvet box and look at some real jewels.

True faith is something like this:

It makes us say yes to life and not run from reality. It will not divide justice from love, nor imagine we can have a credible love for God apart from involvement in pain and the breaking down of barriers that separate. It is not predeterminism. It

Don't Take Any Wooden Emeralds

sets its sights on a world as void of bombs and environmental blight as it has become of polio and smallpox. It does not underestimate the power of forgiveness, or of a God whose central miracle is the gift of life itself. It stands in perpetual amazement at the power of love, and at the fact that every dawn brings reentry into something so awesome no words of mine can begin to touch it.

That's it for me. I hold to a faith that isn't busy trying to prove too many things. James Pike, whose life was as full of contradictions as everyone else's, said what we need is fewer "beliefs" and more "belief." Perhaps that's what Jesus had in mind when he said if you have faith, even as small as a mustard seed, you will be able to order the mountains to move and they will move.

I endorse and proclaim a Christianity that asks for the totality of my life, that wants from me all the talent and excellence I am capable of giving, that rejects any tendency I have to earmark one little niche of self and erect a sign there, one that says, "God, this is the religious me; you can have that."

The part of the Golden State I live in—Southern California—is occasionally panned as a gaudy assortment of substitute everything—a man-made world of asphalt, neon, and plastic impermanence, while Nothern California is thought to be "the place" to be, with its Bay, Lombard Street, fog, and greater sense of style. Granted, Hollywood is in the business of "make believe": "Strike the set; get ready for the next

Accept No Imitations

shot." But wherever we live, for every one of us each day is filled with sorting out the abiding from the transitory. We have to begin again each day to discriminate between the false fronts of movie making and the blue splash of the Pacific Ocean, between the gaudy and the great, the artificial and the abiding.

In the home of my Iowa boyhood, at one end of the dining room, was an oak desk that had a long, shallow central drawer just underneath a fold-down writing shelf. In the drawer was a crazy assortment of junk that looked as though it should be thrown away. Yet no one was ever ready to do that, so its inventory grew rather than diminished. It held trinkets, picture wire, tape measures, rulers, thumbtacks, parade badges, pens with advertising on their sides. I remember spending hours exploring the contents of that remarkable tray. One item never failed to fascinate me, no matter how many times I looked at it, or held it in my hands. It was a small, cone-shaped, irregularly cut rock. I guess it was mica but it looked like a big nugget of platinum or silver. Dad explained though, that it was fool's gold, not worth much of anything at all.

There are times when we like to be fooled. But that is dangerous when it comes to the supreme things in life. There is a difference between life understood as the mindless spin of a wheel of fortune or as the dream of a God who is up to something.

It really isn't a counterfeit world. It is a good world

we live in, created by a God of goodness. But we are left with important distinctions to make and some hard choices.

There are genuine emeralds for sale in Cartagena as well as imitations. And there is real faith out there, operative within and among real persons, in the real towns we live in, in our own very real times. Emeralds, apparently, have fascinated people for thousands of years by their beauty. But so has love. In its purest sense it is as hard to forget as a shooting star in a black desert sky.

Fortran and a Fragrance

You have been closed up in your offices too long. Go to a ballgame. No computer ever hit a home run. Go to a hospital and see life start. Take a walk in the park. No machine can compare to the smile of a pretty girl or the laugh of a child.

—"Letters" column, *Time* magazine

Time magazine's "Man of the Year" for 1982 turned out to be not a man, nor a woman, nor a group of persons (the Freedom Fighters of Europe made it one year, the astronauts another), but a machine.

Should we laugh or cry?

Rock musician John Lennon once surprised us by declaring that the Beatles were more popular than Jesus. He was right at that moment. Today (sorry again!) Jesus is probably stuck with lower ratings than the IBM or Apple computer that offers to figure our taxes, remember a million details, and help Johnny with his arithmetic. Somehow the gospel doesn't seem to have much to do with programming or popularity or applause meters.

Whatever the future may hold, its dazzling array of splendiferous electronic packages, GenEnTech (specializes in genetics research and planning) stock, satellite surveillance systems, and the Jarvik-7 artificial heart are part of everyone's tomorrow.

Fortran and a Fragrance

Yep, the toothpaste is out of the tube, and Lenore's bumper sticker is right: "One Nuclear Bomb Can Ruin Your Whole Day." Even this one headline is enough to make the point: "First Baby from Nobel Sperm Bank Born."

Can faith survive such a dangerous, volatile, unstable world?

Or are we making too big a deal out of what, more soberly viewed, is only one more chapter of change that has gone on since the dawn of history?

After all, faith survived the invention of printing. And electricity. And Freud. And those soft landings on Mars.

One thing looks sure: once cable television and computers become fully interconnected and operational, then 1984 is wholly here, wearing a tiara of triumph on her head and holding a rod of lightning in her hand.

A better question than, Will faith survive? is *What kind* of faith *should* survive? Faith in what? Faith in whom?

Whatever is your answer to that question, an undeniable fact is that kites still rise against the wind, and challenges, whatever their shape, still represent crucibles of greatness.

Wrote the poet Maria Rilke: "How should we be able to forget those ancient myths about dragons that at the last minute turn into princesses who are only waiting to see us once beautiful and brave? Perhaps everything terrible is in its deepest being something helpless that wants our help."

When our family moved to California eighteen years ago, our first home was a house in northwest Los Angeles, up in the hills, a stone's throw from Mount Saint Mary's College. When the skies were clear, we could see the ocean shining in the distance.

Not long after we had gotten settled, it was time for an Academy Awards night, a national cinematic event then being held at the Santa Monica Civic Auditorium. I remember being able, that first April, to look down from our hillside and see the searchlights and floodlights lighting up the southern sky in the vicinity of the auditorium. It seemed as if we had indeed arrived in glamorous California.

Recently, in connection with an Oscar awards ceremony, I heard one expert say, concerning one of the top nominated pictures, *"This one* has the smell of truth about it."

The Bible, too, has the smell of truth about it. That's why it won't leave us alone.

It is, as we know, not a book about perfect people. It isn't one star-spangled paragraph after another about goodness. References to beauty and love are there, but so are frequent mentions of human betrayals and viciousness—Esau's misjudgment of values, Peter's tears, Judas' suicide, demons on the loose, a young man—far from home—wondering why things had turned out so disastrously, just when

Fortran and a Fragrance

it looked like it might have been fun and games forever.

The Bible doesn't trick us, either about ourselves or how the world is made. And, most important of all, it doesn't kid us about God.

It tells us we are more than interesting and complicated specimens of biology—that we are the offspring of God, heirs of the grace of life.

It tells us right and wrong matter, and that even when we seem to be getting by without our integrity being challenged, or without experiencing any clear reward or punishment based on what we do, these issues *still* matter, and while the world sees us on the outside, God looks upon the heart.

The Bible also tells us that beyond our failures, however many they are in number or how serious they seem, hope is never extinguished; there is always the promise of a new beginning.

That Book has the smell of truth about it—the smell of life! It says that when we speak about loving God or take upon ourselves the responsibility of trying to be the friends of God, then we must have the smell of truth about us. If not, there is an odor of deceit.

The apostle Paul once spoke of the influence of the early Christians as a fragrance in the midst of human disorganization and failed intentions.

The circumstances back of his statement were these. Earlier Paul had written an angry letter to the people at Corinth. Then there had been a long silence.

Did that ever happen to you? Did you ever write a letter and fill it with words or feelings or criticisms you felt you just had to divest yourself of? Then did you wait for a shoe to drop, the phone to ring, a reply to show up in the mail? And go half-crazy, wondering what reaction the letter produced in the one who received it? When no word came, you scolded yourself for having written it. You imagined all sorts of things about what it was going to do to your relationship with that person.

Then one day you saw him or her, and a little lump of anxiety welled up inside your throat. But to your great surprise you discovered that, instead of ruining the relationship, it had opened the way to getting something, which had been twisted out of shape, straightened again. And suddenly you felt terribly thankful that things were still okay between you.

That's the way Paul felt—greatly relieved that his letter to the Corinthians had not produced the resentment toward him he was afraid it might have.

For there had come, not a letter of reply, but the arrival of Titus who had been to Corinth, had talked to the people, and had brought a report to Paul that was warmly reassuring. Yes, things were still okay. Paul was still their friend.

So now Paul is smiling again—his emotions at floodtide, celebrating his own happy news, and writing euphorically: "Thanks be to God, who in

Fortran and a Fragrance

Christ always leads us to triumph, and through us spreads the fragrance of the knowledge of him everywhere. For we are the aroma of Christ" (II Cor. 2:14-15a).

Secularity—life without God—frequently seems enough. Who needs God, anyway, as long as one has the bank, modern medicine, and self-help manuals by the ton? Who needs God? Who needs the church as long as life is great sport without it, and there are fourteen better things to do with our time and money? Who needs a Christ when one is a success in his or her profession, when wars are winnable, and the sun shines?

But the questions won't leave us alone.

Our hearts won't leave us alone, either.

We are like the writer of Psalm 42 who prayed, "As a deer longs for a stream of cool water, / so I long for you, O God. / I thirst for you, the living God" (Ps. 42:1-2a TEV).

The Christian faith has an element of surrender in it. I don't challenge that. After we have stated our preferences and done our best, we are, I agree, ready to say, "Your will be done." That was Gethsemane, and it is our prayer, too.

But the Christian faith is also a Star that invites attention more than ordering people about. God is a God of persuasion and that is what makes the modern emphasis on "Process Theology" so interesting. God "rules," it argues, largely by beckoning us, urging us to follow a gleam of light because we love, not because we are subjects, under obligation to comply.

Mary's Christmas prayer was: "Let it happen as you say" (Luke 1:38 Phillips).

And her words find an echo inside of us: let my life, too, find its model and pattern in something that lies beyond iself.

Without some such reference we are mired in that place Judith Viorst parodies in *How Did I Get to Be 40 & Other Atrocities*.

> I've finished six pillows in Needlepoint,
> And I'm reading Jane Austen and Kant,
> And I'm up to the pork and black beans
>   in Advanced Chinese Cooking.
> I don't have to struggle to find myself
> For I already know what I want.
> I want to be healthy and wise and extremely good-looking.
>
> I'm learning new glazes in Pottery Class,
> And I'm playing new chords in Guitar,
> And in Yoga I'm starting to master the lotus position.
> I don't have to ponder priorities
> For I already know what they are:
> To be good-looking, healthy, and wise.
> And adored in addition.
>
> I'm improving my serve with a tennis pro,
> And I'm practicing verb forms in Greek,
> And in Primal Scream Therapy all my frustrations are vented.
> I don't have to ask what I'm searching for
> Since I already know that I seek
> To be good-looking, healthy, and wise.

And adored.
And contented.

I've bloomed in Organic Gardening,
And in Dance I have tightened my thighs,
And in Consciousness Raising there's no one around
  who can top me.
And I'm working all day and I'm working all night
To be good-looking, healthy, and wise.
And adored.
And contented.
And brave.
And well-read.
And a marvelous hostess,
Fantastic in bed,
And bilingual,
Athletic,
Artistic . . .
Won't someone please stop me?

Self-esteem is more than supporting a current self-image.

If that's all it is, what do we do with Jesus?

Faith is rather finding and making connections between our plans and God's—between our ego-hungers and that which is worth naming eternal.

When the danger of forest fires becomes great here in the Southland, which is ordinarily in late July because of dried brush and months without rain, red danger flags go up signaling the people to be especially careful.

It has gotten to be "careful time" for spiritual writers, too, now that we seem to know so much with

Accept No Imitations

our heads, yet remain so uncertain in our souls about what our lives are supposed to mean, or to what we want our energies to be ultimately dedicated.

Silence may be better than simplistic, unworthy answers, so let's not be too hard on our agnostic or purely scientific friends.

Yet faith, boldly redefined, faith that gives birth to vision and courage, is best of all.

The birth of every child begins the world again, and Reinhold Niebuhr was right when he said we have to begin again each day to be Christian. We have nothing to apologize for when asking what faith makes the greatest sense for our time. Life is a moving river, not a motionless statue. And the Holy Spirit never sleeps.

We know that all things are perishable, save God. That part of growing up and growing old involves learning to make peace with death. But the death of *trust* is something else.

Some of our common life has the appearance of being wrapped in permanence, yet turns out not to be. *Life, Collier's,* and the *Saturday Evening Post* disappear. Bing Crosby and Carl Sandburg die, though George Burns defies the law. Our kids grow up and our private worlds have to be reorganized, re-created, and redefined. Someone whom we've never heard of ends up in the White House. Ceylon turns into Sri Lanka. Automobile engines move from the rear to the front. Typewriters go electric, then turn into word processors, which then become something else even more advanced.

Now, high technology has come to make its home with us on a permanent basis. With its wonders, fantastic new good is possible. But we should not allow such new information science to turn us into automatons, sitting at home or at downtown desks pushing buttons, or to produce layers of electronic insulation between the members of the human family.

A woman in a large midwestern city left her suburban apartment one morning for a trip downtown on the bus. She put on one of her most fashionable outfits and her Charlie perfume and headed out the side door to catch Bus #49 that would transport her to one of the best shopping districts.

As she hurried out the door, she had a last-minute thought—to pick up a small sack of garbage that had accumulated in the kitchen and to toss it into the container at the back edge of her property.

But, for some reason, her mental gears shifted, and she forgot she had the garbage, along with other things she was carrying and lugged it unknowingly onto the bus.

As she rode bus #49 through some of the less attractive streets in the city's poorer neighborhoods, she became aware of smells that she didn't particularly like. "Some people just don't know how to live," she said to herself. "They just aren't very clean."

Not until she reached the front door of I. Magnin's

and began to gather her parcels together did she realize where the bad odor was coming from!

That must have been close to what Jesus had in mind when he discussed the religion of the Pharisees. They had the smell of truth about them, but it was not the smell of orange blossoms. It was rather the smell of death.

My fourth grade teacher's name was Vera Smith. She was tall and brunette and kept all of us interested in learning and growing and asking questions. But the thing I remember most about Miss Smith was her lovely smell.

Ultimately, we come out on the fragrance side of some kind of vast equation. We do not deny the horrors of the world we live in. We do not seek escape into the illusion that suffering doesn't exist or that death doesn't, at times, tear our souls to pieces. Neither do we back away from the fact that we are alone, or that there is no hope for tomorrow, or that there is nothing supremely great and good to live for, or die for.

A writer of a magazine article, looking at our times, said editorially, "Something fundamental seems to be missing." That's probably correct. But it is not correct to say that it has been forgotten. It lives in us who still dare to hope.

In a letter to Donatus written seventeen hundred years ago, a man named Cyprian, after describing the behavior of a certain group of persons wrote, "These people, Donatus, are the Christians, and I am one of them."

We call this Good News, and we are dedicated to getting the Word around. The New Testament line that reads "God so loved the world . . . " is rightly called the greatest "so" on earth.

A Piedmont Airlines advertisement in a southern airport invites our business by this phrase, "Own the Sky!"

Maybe that's what faith does for us and with us. It doesn't send us out hunting for some mythological image of God which has little or no meaning to a space-minded, space-traveled generation. But it does remove some old limits. It doesn't make us angels, but it does graft us into a people. It doesn't supply us with all the answers our minds yearn to know. It does give us a foundation for our lives—and a vision. Not a "piece of the rock" (to borrow from another popular commercial) but a piece of the truth that will outlast time itself.

An Educated Heart

As I near the end of my freshman year, I find something is missing from my life. I feel as though I am floating aimlessly through my days, and my nights are lonely. I feel strangely alienated from friends and I am not at peace with myself. Where am I going?

What I would really like is to be able to find God again. I'm not sure how I lost touch, but I do know that I am dissatisfied with living my life without meaning. I don't know where to start except that I would really like to study the New Testament and start helping other people again. I think I will feel better if I can get out of myself. Starting is what is so hard and I am so tired. The plastic smiles and real smiles are so confused in my mind. I know you're very busy, but I need your help. It's raining outside today, but the real storm is raging inside my soul. I am 18 going on 1,000 and I can't go on living like this.

I'll be home June 15. Could I see you then? Kay

One way is to help strangers understand where Claremont, California is on the map is to locate it halfway between Los Angeles and San Bernardino, or to say it lies within the eastern border of L.A. County at the foot of Mt. Baldy. A still better way is to mention its famous Oxford-style colleges—Pomona, Scripps, Harvey Mudd, Claremont McKenna, Pitzer, and the Claremont Graduate School—and to describe it as a mecca for advanced learning. Claremont believes in educating minds.

Educated hearts, though, are as essential as educated minds. That truth is captured in a motto engraved on one of the campus entrances: "Let only the eager, thoughtful and reverent enter here."

In a dream God once asked Solomon, who had inherited the kingship from his father, David, what he would most like to have when assuming his new high office. Solomon answered: "Give therefore thy

An Educated Heart

servant an understanding heart to judge thy people, that I may discern between good and bad: for who is able to judge this thy so great a people?" (I Kings 3:9 KJV). This chapter is about "understanding hearts."

In the mid or late fifties, when Lexington, Kentucky, was my home, the then-president of the U.S., Dwight Eisenhower, made a political visit to the Bluegrass country in connection for his run for reelection. I remember that beautiful May sun-filled morning—the predictable Ike and Mamie motorcade from the airport past the gleaming white fences of Calumet Farm into the business district, finally up to the steps of Morrison Hall, a historic, colonial-type building that is part of Transylvania College. There, the President spoke to a large crowd that had filled adjoining Gratz Park.

The Korean War had at last ended. And, at that point in our national history, Indochina and Vietnam were parts of the world the French knew about and were involved with, but not the Americans. We were, though, part of the Southeast Asia Treaty Organization, and still thought collective security for that part of the planet had some of the same benefits as NATO. But Asia was beginning to unravel. Little did we know the chaos and bewilderment the next few years would bring.

Candidate Eisenhower didn't try to make any pontifical predictions that day, but he did have something terribly meaningful to say, at least to me, about educated hearts.

His subject was the nation. He invited us to develop into a people of character, of moral integrity, and of compassion. Since then his idea seems to have taken on an increasingly personal connotation as, through these intervening years, I have brooded over what a truly educated heart is.

An educated *mind* is easier to define. It's an agile mentality, good SAT scores, a well-furnished vocabulary, a sense of history. It's the knowledge of science and the arts, brilliance, skills, books, facts, the fine arts, questions, answers, biology, math, physics, a knowledge of government. It's philosophy, anatomy, languages, chemistry, and sociology.

But Solomon's prayer, uttered against a background of power and palaces, of wealth and a reputation for wisdom, and other signs of monarchical grandeur, sweeps us into another world of values, into one that has to do with quality of spirit—that leads to a consideration of what we mean by God and those purposes of God that seem to be greater than our own most impressive inventions.

"What I would really like," says the letter in the headnote, "is to be able to find God again." Kay, you speak for us all.

David, Solomon's father, gave us another unforgettable prayer: "Create in me a clean heart, O God, / and put a new and right spirit within me" (Ps. 51:10).

Jesus, in the parable of the soil, spoke about "an honest and good heart" (Luke 8:15).

An Educated Heart

Paul wrote about the light that has "shone in our hearts" because Christ has come (II Cor. 4:6). Peter wrote about a star that rises there even against the darkness of tragedies that look like the clear defeat of goodness (II Pet. 1:19).

But nowhere else in the Bible is there a duplicate of the prayer of the young king that he be given "an understanding heart" to judge the people. The historian who gave us the Books of I and II Kings says Solomon's prayer pleased God.

Someone has said that success means self-esteem, and that it can be a good defense against criticism and lies. It means having friends who are loyal and honest in their criticism, laughing at ourselves, feeling pain when someone is in trouble, seeing the good in others and in ourselves, and living with our shortcomings. The abundance of the invisible.

An educated heart, I have concluded, has something to do with inward freedom. It means we have identified something within ourselves to rely on and something outside of ourselves to care about and live for. To have found or acquired these is to have earned a bachelor's degree of the Spirit.

Such a heart also has a guest room—it isn't complete in itself and knows it isn't. It knows its own limits. Modesty of achievement almost always characterizes those whose ability has taken them to the tops of their fields. Without lapsing into self-doubt or self-contempt, they still are ready to acknowledge that the more they know, the more they are in awe both of the universe and of mysteries still unexplained.

So Kay's problems and those of our whole civilization are, in one sense, the same:

These are hard directives
Sometimes, God—

To run and not be weary,
To walk and not faint.

Today tears came;
There seemed to be no end,
A catharsis of
Strung-together days of
Sub-strength,
Sub-accomplishment.

My emotions just do not square
With my dreams, my standards.
They register apathy,
Futility, fear,
Disappointment.

They say,
"You have blown
Great opportunities."
They say,
"You are going nowhere."

Yet you say,
"Trust in the Lord and
He will give you the
Desires of your heart."

An Educated Heart

I must take the steps
To pray and to move,
Even when my emotions are
Out of sync.

Jane A. Peterson

Educated hearts are not arrogant hearts. They are "understanding" because they *stand under* some large, enduring truth. For some, that may stay nameless. For me, it is the God who speaks to me in Jesus Christ. God is the one who claims my life and loves me out of whatever feelings of unworthiness or frustration threaten me with a sense of meaninglessness or failure.

It's an opening baseball play-off game between Baltimore and California, and everyone in these parts is hugely excited. After nineteen years, the Angels, an expansion club, have at last made it to the big time. And they desperately want to do well. So, when one of their best hitters, Grich or Baylor, stands up at the plate and hits the ball in a way that causes it to soar on a high, long arc into the outfield, a cry of joy goes up in Anaheim. Maybe the team *will* go all the way this time! The ball, though long enough, could wind up foul instead of fair. It's hit well enough to be a glorious home run. But is the ball fair or foul? God, let it be fair!

Announcer Dick Engberg is as turned-on as anyone else, but sadly, must report, "Foul!"

Said Dick, "These Angel fans *watched that one with their hearts.*"

His phrase tumbled about in my head for two weeks, and I kept reading into it something deeper.

Then one afternoon, as I walked along a pleasant street on a sunny July morning, a line from the Ephesian letter broke through to me and helped me realize that watching something with one's heart isn't a new idea.

I remembered a prayer that Paul included in a letter to one of those first-century congregations. He prayed that God would give the people wisdom and that—listen—*"having the eyes of your hearts enlightened,* you may know what is the hope to which he [God] has called you" (Eph. 1:18, italics added).

We do *see* with our hearts.

A young woman falls in love with a young man. The parents can't figure out the attraction. The guy doesn't look all that handsome or promising. But they do not see what she sees. She *sees* him with her heart.

A college girl named Bev, whose home is in San Rafael, goes to school several hundred miles away and battles with homesickness. Home for Christmas, she tells her mother, as they ride along in the family car, how much she missed home and her familiar surroundings during those first weeks and months away. As she reaches the climax of her confession, the car tops a rise and the Golden Gate Bridge looms in front of them. In the distance, the lights of San Francisco begin to twinkle on. She grasps her mother's sleeve as she gazes toward the city and says, "Oh, Mother, *see* what I mean!"

No one can *prove* Jesus is the Messiah. No one can prove Jerusalem is anything more than an old walled city with a reputation for conflict among the religious and political forces of the Middle East, that the Sea of Galilee is anything more than a body of water, that the Holy Spirit is anything more than subjective imagination, or that the church is anything more than another loyalty-seeking institution—*unless* one watches history with one's heart—unless one makes the leap of faith and takes the risk of being wrong.

Pulpit great Ralph Sockman once wrote about "hospitality to the highest." That's what an educated heart offers. It's what a genuine nation is open to.

I'll never forget once being asked, in my first parish, to help a family in which a thirty-four-year-old university professor with a Ph.D. had suddenly taken his life. Suicide is a complicated phenomenon to attempt to explain or rationalize. But I can't forget my startledness that a young man of obvious brilliance with reasonable health and two nice kids did not have something in all of his training to fall back upon when the desperate moments came.

Later I visited a big drug rehabilitation hospital and discovered that a number of the patients there were medical doctors. I was startled again.

Gradually I learned a lesson. Life is more than a contest of ideas with all the blue chips winding up in the hands of the clever, the shrewd, the bright, the brainy.

If I had bothered to read the Book of Proverbs more closely, I would have known that. Of if I had probed more deeply the words of Jesus that have to do with the sort of treasures that do not grow old and that do not wear out, I would have known that.

We get offered so much. There's so much for sale. So much to do. We are importuned to be physically fit, to travel the globe, dress in style, become well educated, attend the theater, get the best interest on our savings, and the most out of our sexuality.

Those are not ignoble ambitions, but life is more than consumption.

There is a familiar note of tragedy in a speech one of the characters in William Golding's novel *Free Fall* (Harcourt Brace Jovanovich, 1962) makes to another character:

> There is no health in you, Mr. Mountjoy. You do not believe in anything enough to suffer for it or be glad. There is no point at which something has knocked on your door and taken possession of you. You possess yourself. Intellectual ideas, even the idea of loyalty to your country, sit on you loosely. You wait in a dusty waiting room in no particular line for no particular train.

We can have good muscle tone and plenty in the bank and still be beggars in velvet, lacking both a zest for the world as it is or a dream of what Jesus Christ challenges it to be.

An educated heart has this, too, which helps define

it: it cares about others; it is not indifferent or neutral about the pain of others; and it never stops asking questions. It has room for those who knock on its door or for those who are too sick or tired to knock on anyone's door, but whose survival even so is in our hands. And it never gives up its search for the genuine, the real, the treasure hidden in a field.

And educated hearts know something special about time. They recognize flashdances of truth in words like these:

> Come now, you who say, "Today or tomorrow we will go into such and such a town and spend a year there and trade and get gain." Whereas you do not know about tomorrow. What is your life? For you are a mist that appears for a little time and then vanishes. Instead you ought to say, "If the Lord wills we shall live and shall do this or that." (James 4:13-15)

Or, in words of Psalm 90: "So teach us to number our days that we may get a heart of wisdom" (v. 12).

Or Ecclesiastes: "He hath made every thing beautiful in his time: also he hath set the world in their heart" (Eccles. 3:11 KJV).

Educated hearts don't take much for granted. Instead, they see all existence in terms of gift, all of life in terms of stewardship, all hours as holy.

Evelyn Whitehead in *Christian Life Patterns* (Doubleday & Co., 1979) says Christians are "prepared to discover God's active presence within the surprising and often painful crises and transitions of adult life . . . are surprised and grateful to be graced with the strengths that allow them to love well and to care for what they and others have generated."

A truly educated heart would also endorse this rendition of the Beatitudes, created by a group of Franciscans:

> People who do not hold tightly to things are happy
> because all of God's kingdom is theirs.
> People who are gentle with the earth
> will see it blossom forever.
> People who can cry for all the world's suffering
> will live to see happiness.
> People who hunger and thirst for what is right
> will finally have their fill.
> People who really care
> will find love wherever they go.
> People who won't let the world get them down
> will see God.
> People who make peace happen
> are God's children.
> People who give up their own comfort so that others
> can be helped
> know what heaven is all about.
> Lord, let us be like these!

When Israel was looking for a leader to replace Saul, the people depended on Samuel's judgment. It was not easy for him to make a choice. At first, one candidate, Eliab, seemed to have all the right qualifications. But Samuel, as he pondered his recommendation, seemed to hear another voice—one that said, "Pay no attention to how tall and handsome he is. I have rejected him, because I do not judge as man judges. Man looks at the outward appearance, but I look at the heart" (I Sam. 16:7 TEV).

Each of us has a heart.

Each of us is a heart.

Together, we are the human heart. Together we share responsibility for becoming a world that knows how to love, to share, to create, and to live in peace.

Amadeus and the Gospel

He was the one who most eloquently spoke of the gap between what life makes of us and what we wanted to be, perhaps what we are still, at one unreachable, diamond-hard core deep inside ourselves.

—James Moore, a reference to Tennessee Williams

There's more to the stage play *Amadeus* than I either understood or have time to write about, but I don't think I missed its main theological point.

It is set in the late eighteenth century in Salzburg, Austria, and the chief character is a man who was also very real in life, Antonio Salieri, a professional musician and composer who, more than anything else in the world, wanted to write great music and be remembered for it. Salieri was a man with a goal that was almost obsessive, and he worked hard to achieve it. He prayed for success, and he pulled all the political levers he could get his hands on to make his dream come true.

But he had a young rival, Wolfgang Amadeus Mozart, who was, or seemed to be, as frivolous as Salieri was serious about writing music.

Mozart was undisciplined, not very exemplary in his morals or language. In the play he gave the

Amadeus and the Gospel

impression of being naïve in politics, not very religious, not very responsible.

In *Amadeus*, Mozart's drinking gets out of hand, his wife leaves him, and his health fails. All the time, Salieri, who wants to but can't be all things his foolish young competitor is musically, struggles his way mechanically and unimaginatively through the scale while free-spirited Mozart is able to create the music of angels, getting his notes perfect the first time.

Salieri turns into a nasty, jealous, prematurely old man who uses all the cunning he can think of to discredit this popular young musician. He is sufficiently successful so that when *The Magic Flute* is ready to be played for the first time, Mozart has to perform it in a beer hall rather than in a concert hall.

Salieri also takes his case to God. He points out to God that he is the virtuous one who deserves to be rewarded. He is the one who works hard, who prays, who knows his craft. He is intelligent, responsible, moral, religious—and desperate, desperate to compose music that will turn out to be immortal.

So Wolfgang Amadeus Mozart accommodates him. He dies, leaving the stage of musical attention to the older man, and for thirty-two more years Salieri writes. And for his works he has medals pinned upon his chest. He gets the polite recognition his ego craves. But in his heart he knows it is the music of Mozart—Wolfgang Amadeus Mozart, who gave the world *The Marriage of Figaro*, and *Don Giovanni*, and concertos and operas so utterly sublime in their beauty that they seem destined to be played and sung as long as the earth lasts—it is *his* music that endures.

Salieri's music perishes almost as soon as it is written. At one point, he says that he is apparently doomed to be the patron saint of mediocrity.

How do we account for such gifts given to the irresponsible?

Grace is the word that describes the unexpected, the undeserved, the charismatic, whether that be in the form of an incredible musical talent, the gift of a child, the looks of a Grace Kelly, or the peace that passes understanding.

Forgiveness and relief when our hearts break—that's grace, too.

Or exoneration from an old mistake that, at times, threatens to tear our lives to bloody shreds and leave our identity as decent human beings in ruins.

The meaning of all these is the same—it is God's love, God's inreach, God's endowment that defies our systems of merit and proves to us over and over how much of life is gift and how little of it is our own doing.

Robert McAfee Brown in his book *Creative Dislocation* (Abingdon Press, 1980) speaks of grace—at least one expression of it—as "creative surprise":

> a stranger walks into one's life and a friendship abides;
>
> a chance encounter is the initiation of a series of planned encounters and a marriage of thirty-six years' duration results;
>
> a piece of music is first heard by the chance spinning of a

radio dial or a randomly selected phonograph record or because someone happened to play that piece and not another—and it beomes an instrument of healing in subsequent times of spiritual fever.

Maybe John Lennon put it best when he said that life is what happens to us while we are busy making other plans.

What we need to get straight is that grace doesn't have only one meaning; it has many. What they all have in common is this: God's actions often supersede our own. Despite our cleverness and wit, or hard work, or attempts to justify ourselves by our own achievements or goodness, designing ways to make up for our sins, it is upon God, not upon ourselves, that our hope for salvation depends. "By grace you have been saved through faith; and this is not your own doing, it is the gift of God" (Eph. 2:8).

Justification by merit appears to make more sense. It sounds fairer. It is more in keeping with the American spirit. We do right; God does right by us. Virtue pays off. Hard work is rewarded, as it should be.

That is why Salieri was mad at God—the system of fairness and predictability didn't and wouldn't work. If it did, the Pharisees would have wound up in heaven with front seats. But we are not the marketers or the managers of the favor of God. And we do not answer questions one through fifteen correctly, then say, "All right, God, I've met your requirements; come through with my 'A.'"

Grace means we can't earn our salvation or

acceptance by God, or treat God's approval as something we are entitled to. It means *gift*. The grace of the Lord Jesus Christ—those words that so often make up the benediction at the end of worship—mean that God *is* the Redeemer who stands in between the righteousness of perfection and our own incompleteness and sin.

The Bible takes sin, alienation, and isolation seriously. That is what gives elegance and power to the meaning of grace. If sin isn't all that big a deal—sin understood as a failure to live up to our divine potential as children of God and as sisters and brothers of one another—then grace also will fail to impress.

Dr. J. Harold Ellens, a Michigan psychologist-theologian, raises the question, What does grace have to do with health and wholeness?

For one thing, he says, it heals, and we all need healing. It gives life dignity, hope, and reductions in stresses that are fed by our own perfectionism and by some of the pressure the world puts upon us to shape up or ship out. It rescues us from loneliness and a sense of having failed and helps us, through an encounter with Jesus Christ, to experience life as celebration.

Grace cleanses. Grace empowers.

Grace brings us down to size and *up* to size.

In *God's Grace and Human Health* (Abingdon Press, 1982) Dr. J. Harold Ellens says, "It is a revealing clinical and biblical fact that people who can be grateful can be healthy and people who are incapable of generating spontaneous and authentic gratitude are unable to be healthy."

Grace enables us to accept unanswered questions of our lives as reminders of our creatureliness and to substitute hope and faith for anger and cynicism. It enables us to deal with the future—to know that *some* of the responsibility for creating and becoming that future is on our shoulders, but not all. And we can say the same for most of the personal decisions we must make—sometimes do make, with trembling.

Dr. Ellens continues, "Nietzsche said the courage to be . . . is the ability to stand at the brink of the abyss of nothingness and hear without flinching the announcement that God is dead."

Ellens has a better word. "The real story . . . is that the courage to be, in this fractured and alienated world, is the abilty to stand in the middle of hopelessness of human alienation and hear the announcement that God has embraced us in spite of ourselves and realize that if God is for us no one can be against us."

There's one line in *Amadeus* I can't precisely recall, but it is to the effect that God used Mozart to "sneak himself into the world." Clearly that is what God did in a schema as surprising and non-obvious as the cross and Jesus dying there for, as the church came to believe, "our sakes."

God also uses each of us as instruments and endows

us in different ways for love's tasks. We may imagine that what grace has conferred on us is not all that crucial or convincing, that the big thing is effort and try, try again. But we're probably wrong there, as we tend to be about many things where God is concerned.

"Grace," said my friend Lofton Hudson once, "is not a blue-eyed blonde." But Lofton could be wrong about that. Maybe that's grace's most persuasive evidence of all—persons!

And it always represents some kind of repudiation of a *quid pro quo* life-style.

Surely Mahatma Gandhi, whose life has leapt back onto the stage of our awareness here in the mid-eighties because of Richard Attenborough's best-picture-of-the-year film, was one of those who pushed back the edge of the dark—even if only a little. In one of the film clips shown the night the Oscars were awarded, we saw him toward the end of his life, still pleading for a way to break the cycle of reciprocal violence, because he knew it was possible if the world made up its mind so to do. He was talking to a Hindu who was guilt-stricken because in the context of some religious violence, he had killed a Muslim child. Gandhi's counsel to the man was to find another lad—about so tall (he gestured)—someone like his son, someone without a father, and help that boy grow up. And he added, "To raise him as a Muslim."

So we can praise God for those who ask of us

seemingly impossible things—who stand as a rebuke to those who insist that you can't change history, that you cannot stop war, or that you cannot change people—that you must come to terms with the world as it is because the world isn't ready for your dream.

Part of the gospel is that we are called out of life as it is, to disturb the universe, even if ever so slightly, to change it from the way we found it.

Each Christmas I take down W. H. Auden's play, *For the Time Being,* and reread those same magnificent words he puts on the lips of the shepherds:

> Music and sudden light
> Have interrupted our routine tonight,
> And swept the filth of habit from
>   our hearts.

Of Paul and Silas it was said by a street mob, "These men who have turned the world upside down have come here also" (Acts 17:6).

Sometimes tragedy turns our worlds upside down, and we have to find a way to hang in, to survive, to grow through what we suffer. Someone has named these experiences "adventures in darkness."

But we don't have to wait for life to rearrange destiny, forcing us to comply or adjust. As the people of the Way we can be initiators of change, people who are ready to be embarrassed to the glory of God by trying to obey a higher law than any the world has gotten used to.

Jesus made waves in several respects. He challenged the accepted divisions among the so-called good and the bad people of his time. He believed that goodness was not so much a matter of externals as it was of purity of heart. He even had a few bad things to say about prayer—where it is done for show or to impress others.

He forces us to "reexamine the criteria" (that's the phrase Richard Attenborough keeps using)—contemporary criteria of weakness and power, and Gandhi's cross shows us a power greater than guns or gold.

When he talked with his disciples that last night on earth, Jesus said to them, "Don't be afraid. God's purposes may be hard to understand, but they will be realized even through my death. Do not cry. I will see you again."

In this country we are proud of the fact that we are not chained to the past. We believe in an "open future." We believe the nation must never stop reforming its life or dreaming giant, new dreams that have to do not only with *our* tomorrows but also with a better world for everyone. And—hallelujah—most of us know that any version of a future America that deserves to be called great, or that is deserving of perpetuity, must be made out of spirit as well as out of science. Which means we must address ourselves to the quality of that future as well as to its efficiency. We must ask God again what we are to do with a wealth and pool of intellectual talent as splendid as ours is.

Sometimes when I talk to people about faith, they tell me that they were soured on religion as children. They didn't like the boredom, the stiffness, the hypocrisy. The church was a "turn off," a waste of time, unrelated to the more tactile world of money, power, machinery, and martinis. Well, I don't want anything to do with dead religion either, or false gods. But, without God, I cannot make sense either of the world or of myself, and I prefer not to settle for less than emeralds.

One of the most influential people in my life was a man named Jesse Halsey. It was he who served as my most believable model of what a Christian pastor could mean to others. For twenty-nine years he pastored the Seventh Presbyterian Church in Cincinnati. It was his recommendation to a church in Kentucky that resulted in my answering a call to that congregation in the fall of 1953. When I experienced great mental distress over leaving the Iowa church which had first called me and given me my first pulpit gown and my first chance to prove myself as a preacher and church leader, Dr. Halsey, from Chicago where he was living, scrawled a letter in which he quoted Paul: "Forgetting what lies behind and reaching forward to what lies ahead, let us press on toward the prize of the upward call of God in Christ Jesus." He underlined the words "reaching forward to what lies ahead." Those are words we all

Accept No Imitations

have to underline at times for ourselves when we have encountered or lived through a tough and demanding human experience. (You'll find these words in Philippians, chapter 3.)

When a young man, Dr. Halsey once did some volunteer work in Labrador with one of the great missionary physicians of the first half of the twentieth century, Dr. Wilfred Grenfell. Later Dr. Grenfell wrote of the young preacher from Southampton, "I have seen more of Jesus Christ in him than in anyone I ever knew."

When I arrived in Lexington and sat down to work out plans for the service of installation, Dr. Halsey was the first person I thought about, the one I most wanted to be there. But when I called long distance, Mrs. Halsey gave me the news: "Dr. Halsey died two days ago, but he said a few days before that he wanted you to know he wished great things for you there in your new work."

Jacob found God's goodness in his brother Esau and in his brother's readiness to forgive him of earlier cheating him out of his birthright. "To see your face is like seeing the face of God," he told him out there on the desert when they met each other after not seeing each other for many years.

With that kind of faith, we turn into conquerors indeed.

Peace Yes, Freedom Yes

Let us be called the children of God,
speaking boldly with moral conviction to the nation
and to the world,
building, with God's grace, a new moral order in the
world community; and
acting now for world peace, an enterprise of justice, an
outcome of love.

—Peacemaking: The Believer's Calling

In the closing scene of Herman Wouk's *The Winds of War* (Little, Brown, 1971), Navy Captain Victor Henry stands at dawn on a high rock escarpment outside Pearl Harbor watching an aircraft carrier steam eastward. It has been a couple of months now since the December 7, 1941, Japanese attack, and it will be another year before the American fleet can represent a serious counterforce in the Pacific. Still, it is important to put to sea with what remains of the battered inventory of the Pacific detachments of the United States Navy to avoid the appearance of having been fatally downed.

The captain's son, Warren, is aboard the *Enterprise* as it navigates cautiously through the channel below. Warren has qualified as a navy flyer and will soon be flying himself through curtains of heavy flak, his chances of dying equally as great as his chances for survival.

Accept No Imitations

The captain, already war weary from assignments in Berlin and London, turns his face

> to the indigo arch of the sky, where Venus and the brightest stars still burned. . . . He could almost picture God the Father looking down with sad wonder at this mischief. In a world so rich and lovely, could his children find nothing better to do than dig iron from the ground and work it into vast grotesque engines for blowing each other up? Yet this madness was the way of the world.

Peace has become the transcends-all-others issue in these final years of the twentieth century.

Today our capacity for killing is as much more advanced over World War II as digital devices are over old pull-crank adding machines, or the space shuttle is over the P-38. Sophisticated long and short-range missiles, continental knockout power housed inside the hull of submarines—all this has produced a debate over survivability which I don't expect to see resolved in my lifetime.

Though the Soviet newspaper *Pravda* may not be the best place to turn for factual information, I couldn't help wincing at one of its stories that was reproduced locally in which a report on Afghanistan stated that four years of war there now have resulted in the destruction of 1,804 schools, 143 hospitals and health centers, and 25,000 miles of road and rail lines.

Today, scientists discuss the potential destruction of the whole world as earnestly and with as much fear as was once used only by radio evangelists with their index finger touching one of the sentences in the Revelation of Saint John.

Armageddon-style war, with estimated casualties listed in the millions, has, like Pac-Man, tended to gobble up almost every other human consideration in the Book of Knowledge. The massacre of the race. The end of everything. The price of the American military "answer"—a million dollars a minute.

And peace is not primarily a leftover issue from Vietnam or a political topic having to do mainly with the Middle East. It's the top question that outranks every other question.

Yet, it is not the *only* question, or the only concern we have about the future if there is to be one.

Over the past several centuries when the world was forced to make a choice between slavery and a battlefield it has, in most instances, chosen the battlefield. People have preferred both to fight and to die in order to hang onto such freedoms as have been wrought out of uncountable old power contests and assaults upon the human spirit. Aleksandr Solzhenitsyn speaks of this as the slim thread of "moral nerve" by which civilization hangs suspended, and he argues that if we put survival ahead of this crucial value, the most important thing about us is dead already.

Is the present choice analogous?

Many say it is not.

Accept No Imitations

They point out that the devastation of the world by nuclear war cannot "save freedom," no matter how ideally motivated or how many die on behalf of such a cause. They ask, How can we discuss this as "a choice"?

Such a point of view may be correct, but I don't want us to stop talking about freedom as we sometimes have done or to separate peace from freedom any more than we are willing to separate peace and justice.

There are still values worth dying for if dying can keep them alive. But maybe dying won't. Maybe all the sacrifices of all the brave women and men in the world who are willing to make them won't be enough. And the end result may be only smoke and ashes, loneliness, the death even of memory. Yet we know that freedom always has been, always will be, a costly affair.

How can we affirm, support, be wise enough to honor the message and urgent cry of today's peace movement and at the same time remain resistant to those who would rob us of the right to be or stay free? Is it possible? Or has history moved into a new phase of cosmic danger that makes the question unaskable?

I want to be a peacemaker. I want a safe human society to live in. I want to see the Genevas won, the world disarmed, the cross of iron lifted off the backs of all countries, large and small. A replacement B-52 bomber costs $285 million. One airplane! Enough to feed one of the smaller nations for two years!

Peace Yes, Freedom Yes

But I want to keep another flame alive, too! If you ask me how big a price I am ready to pay for that, or how large a risk I am willing to run to try to keep freedom from dying, another set of Dark Ages from beginning, I can't answer. The spectre of full-scale nuclear war is so immoral and so dreadful that it can't be treated as a bargaining chip. Still peace and freedom belong together as parents to a child or light and water to a tree.

And we mustn't wait too long. Or leave the outcome to blind fate. We must become vocal, active peacemakers on whatever terms square with our own hearts and sense of right.

After his wife died, Thomas Carlyle wrote, "If I just had you by my side five minutes longer; I would tell you everything!" But Carlyle knew it could not be. It was too late to say even one more time: "I love you." Too late.

On Bunker Hill, in downtown Los Angeles, there was an apartment fire that took the lives of two people. The newspaper story said it was an instance where a smoke detector would certainly have saved them. Days later, another story let us know that smoke detectors would now be installed throughout all those apartment buildings.

A familiar case of deja vu. Too late to help those who perished, but maybe the lesson gained will help others in the future.

It was 1930, and Eric Sevareid, a budding young journalist, was in Germany. In Oberammergau, the picturesque Alpine village where the story of Christ is acted out every ten years on a massive stage, Sevareid wandered into a gift shop one day and found on display a sign with the words: "No Jews Allowed."

This struck him as incongruous. To see in Oberammergau, world famous for telling and retelling to the world the story of the Prince of Peace, the One of whom Paul wrote: "He is our peace who has made us both one, and has broken down the dividing wall of hostility" (Eph. 2:14)—a sign reading, "No Jews."

He asked the shopkeeper, a kind-faced woman who appeared to be wholly without hate and who probably had never fired a gun in her life—whose main interests undoubtedly were her family, her health, the simple concerns of village people—why she would have a sign like that in her shop?

She answered with a quaver: "We can do nothing about it. We are helpless. We only do what we are told by the police."

Too late now. Our destiny is in the hands of others. The time to resist is past. Too late. Too late.

Former governor of California Jerry Brown, in connection with his unsuccessful candidacy for the presidency, described what he thought peace would look like if it came marching down the street. He spoke of a human order that would protect the earth, serve the people, and explore the universe.

All that is possible without war.

Peace Yes, Freedom Yes

But the threat to freedom and independence of life—ah, that's where the going gets tough indeed, for all these things are commendable, if we are not standing in the shadow of someone whose lust for power threatens to destroy the self-governing society we have built upon these shores we call America.

Since Vietnam we have been terribly conscious of defects in our own national character. We need to be careful, when identifying the threats to peace, that we do not rule ourselves out of the equation. We now fully know and admit that we are part of the problem as well as part of the answer. Yet we also are a people with a grand idealism and the virtue of self-criticism. To ignore the trusteeship of freedom that we believe has been partly committed to our care and preservation would be as bad as to ignore our own complicity in wrong.

My bike was stolen. Afterward I did what I learned all of us have to do after such experiences, go to the police station storage shed and see if it has been found.

The first time I went to ask if the police had found it on some nearby street, or somewhere else in their investigations, it wasn't there. The second time I went, it was.

But I hardly recognized it. The front wheel was gone. The leather seat was gone. The back wheel was there, but bent out of shape. The bike wasn't even worth taking home. I did, however, load it into the trunk anyway and take it back to our garage.

As I looked at the wrecked frame, labeled the "Free Spirit" model, I found myself thinking that this must be the way the world looks to God—a wheel missing, broken gears, scratched paint—a planet divided, bent under the burden of hate, mistrust, blackmail, spoilation, and an arsenal of weapons so big and destructive that we can hardly find words enough to describe it.

Yet God claims it, loves it. Even if a bomb should be detonated and almost totally abolish organized life, God would still be on hand, playing the part of the wounded healer.

We need to do all we can for peace before it is too late; we need to concern ourselves with *means* as well as with ends. We should not let ourselves come to the place in which the shopkeeper in Oberammergau found herself when she said to Eric Sevareid, "We are helpless; it's in someone else's hands now."

We *can* be instruments of change, helping one another know that God affirms us, forgives us, and loves us out of what we have been into a new world of becoming where our anxiety levels are reduced and where there is peace. As Christians we are not burdened with having to prove to anyone that we are good. We know that we are not, but that our ungoodness does *not* mean we are not persons of value and beauty, the center of God's heart. We know we are.

Peace Yes, Freedom Yes

We need to make peace with yesterday. But just as important we need to make peace with the unknown, uncontrollable future. If part of the problem of the past is grief over what we have lost or regret over what we should have done, the problem of the future is worry over what might happen.

To that, faith also addresses a word of confidence. We must do our best to help create the future and to spread the news that God is Lord of the future.

> I know not what the future hath
> Of marvel or surprise,
> Assured alone that life and death
> God's mercy underlies.
>
> John Greenleaf Whittier

The Christian Century carried an article about those who make their religious millions by warning the rest of us that the end of the world is around the corner, always taking care to assure us that this is precisely what the Bible has predicted. That's exploitative, cruel theology. The theology of the Scriptures is God's call to us to follow in the paths of peace, "to do justly, and to love mercy, and to walk humbly with thy God" (Mic. 6:8 KJV)—to love our neighbors as ourselves. And I do not believe that God has some fiery Grand Finale out there just waiting so the Scriptures can be fulfilled on some kind of divine schedule or foreordained timetable. God is judge as well as redeemer, but God is also our redeemer as well as our judge, and God's power is the power of life, not destruction.

In the January 19, 1983, issue of *The Christian Century*, Lloyd J. Averill, who lives in Kalamazoo, Michigan, wrote:

> Perhaps the end of the world *is* near. I don't know what foolish things people and nations will permit themselves to do in the near future, what compacts we will make with hell through the use of nuclear and biological weapons, what ecological disasters we will actively perpetrate or merely permit to happen or what unprecedented human tragedy we will willingly or witlessly sponsor. I only know that if there is a danger of the imminent destruction of the world, God's hand is not in it. And if I am to be God's man for this moment, it will be my obligation to work with him to see that it doesn't happen.

On a more personal level, we do well to remind ourselves still one more time that the God of our worship is the God of hope. We are sustained by that hope. We cannot know the future and cannot regulate it, but we can trust it, love it, believe in it.

If we will, we can avoid Armageddon, just as we have rid the world of typhus and witchcraft and signs that once read, "Whites Only," or "We Reserve the Right to Refuse Service to Anyone."

The place of women is now in the House and the Senate. So far no one pretends to own the moon.

And the world of science and art and biblical scholarship, of Olympic games and human creativity and worship, resists divisions that keep people apart or insist that one group is superior or brighter than another.

Maybe war *is* on its way out.

Maybe love and trust and God will win in the end.

And out of the vineyard will come the fruit of joy, the champagne of peace, a toast to all generations still to come to play the game of life.

Singleness and Marriage— A Double Celebration

The church comes under the judgment of God and invites rejection when it fails to lead men and women into the full meaning of life together, or withholds the compassion of Christ from those caught in the moral confusion of our time.

—*The Confession of 1967* of the Presbyterian Church (U.S.A.)

Everyone has a favorite song and I'll confess to mine. It's one Mary sings in *Jesus Christ Superstar* as she says of Jesus, "I don't know how to love him."

It's not in the same class with "All Hail the Power" or the "Hallelujah Chorus," and may not suit a service of worship, but it's gorgeous just the same.

Superstar made us think of Jesus, not in detached terms of stained-glass divinity or sermons by the seashore, but as a man deeply capable of human love, even romantic love.

Yet he remained a single man, someone who was asked many questions about the meaning of marriage.

We wish we might have known him at twenty-one or twenty-four or twenty-seven. Yet those years between twelve and thirty are a blank. The writings that have tried to fill in our knowledge have never been looked upon as anything more than fictional improvisations—stories invented more to satisfy curiosity than to report the truth. But the fact that Jesus was single, and that he stayed so to his death, is not ordinarily doubted.

Moses was married. So were Abraham, Ruth, Saul, and David. Solomon had seven hundred wives. Most of the prophets apparently were not married, though the Bible says Ezekiel was, and we are told about Ezekiel's grief at the time of his wife's death.

Hosea was married, but his wife left him. Out of all that, he made a parable of the harlotry of Israel and the faithfulness of God.

Peter was married. We know that was true because Jesus visited in Peter's home and his mother-in-law was there. She was ill with a fever. Jesus touched her brow and she became better.

Paul, though, was single. So was Luke. So was Barnabas.

Married or single seems to have had little to do with the special uses God has made of persons as the human story has unfolded.

What sense can we make of the new social attitudes that have emerged and are still forming about both of these states—marriage and singleness? Is there anything in Scripture that provides us with Christian perspective and a way of understanding as to how we ought to think and live?

It's hard not to be defensive. If someone is a single adult, the question asked often seems to hang suspended in midair, How come you're single?

And if the individual is married, the question becomes, I wonder how he and his wife, or she and her husband, are getting along, or, Will it last?

We can learn to think and feel positively about both life-styles.

Marriage is gift. It is a way both to give and to receive love, offering life-corporate dimension. When children are born, we are given a foretaste of the meaning of immortality. A child's birth can be psychologically rewarding as well as demanding—offering a way for people to escape self-centeredness and to know many ecstatic forms of joy.

But singleness is also gift, and everyone lives at least part of his or her adult life as a single person. For all of us there is singleness at the beginning. For many, there is reentry into singleness after a divorce or a death. For some, all of life is lived in the single mode. As part of singleness, there may result freedoms, career possibilities that shine with unusual excellence, or other achievements that simply are not possible on any other terms.

Some would like to marry, but life doesn't work out that way. Others yearn to be unmarried, but life doesn't work out that way, either.

But we shouldn't feel sorry for one another. Whether we are married, single, or divorced doesn't tell the world much about us or about the quality of relationships that we have with others.

Here is the Christian ethic, stated as plainly as I have seen it:

Singleness and Marriage—A Double Celebration

> We declare that marriage and family life,
> while not essential for authentic personhood,
> are good gifts of God.
> A loving home should be the birthright of every child.
>
> We declare that the sexual union of human beings can be a
> pure, joyous, and potent event.
> God forbids us to abuse this gift
> by dominating, hurting, betraying, or using each other.
>
> We affirm the value of love and faithfulness
> and the disaster of lust and faithlessness
> in all our relationships as men and women.
>
> Whether single, bereaved, divorced, or married,
> all are members of the human family.
>
> From *A Declaration of Faith*—Proposed Book of Confessions, 1974. The Presbyterian Church of the United States, now part of the Presbyterian Church (U.S.A.)

Fortunately, we have entered a different time when most of us are glad to be rid, once and for all, of the sin of not acknowledging singles as fully franchised persons. And, praise heaven, divorce is no longer, for most of us, the life-wrecking stigma that cripples and blocks the arrival of fresh tomorrows and those new beginnings that are integral to the church's message of hope.

Matthew writes: "And Pharisees came up to him and tested him by asking, 'Is it lawful to divorce one's wife for any cause?' " (19:3).

Note these are the Pharisees who were the great

legalists, highly religious, terribly strict, piously noisy, offensively self-righteous. And Matthew says that back of their question was a desire to "test" Jesus, to embarrass him or to corner him, to expose him as someone willing to play fast and loose with canon law.

But Jesus was not a legalist. Everything in the New Testament supports that statement. Whether the subject was sabbath observances, divorce laws, or the payment of taxes, he always appears ready to put people ahead of principles, love ahead of law.

"Is it *lawful* to divorce one's wife?"

Although Jesus' answer has often been read by church lawyers in the past as edict—a Supreme Court opinion on what God approves and what God does not approve—what his reply really means is that marriage needs to be entered into as a sacred business, dissolved only where there seems to be no other way out. And he goes on to say that you can't always settle things by rules. Not all arrangements fit all people in the same way.

By way of illustration, Jesus refers to what the Bible describes as eunuchs. These usually were men who acted as servants, doorkeepers, or cupbearers, persons who exercised considerable authority but were rendered impotent to make sure they were not sexual threats within a large household. Jesus says that, for some of these, such service is noble, and they are happy in what they are doing. But, and here he speaks in effect to the Pharisees who asked the question, "You probably wouldn't look upon that way of life as acceptable to you at all. So don't try to make all people the same. And don't imagine all marriages are the same. Divorce is an accommodation to a splendid ideal. So is life."

Singlehood and marriagehood are occasions for affirmation and celebration if—

1. We don't put the two in opposition to each other. If we avoid another form of segregation as contrary to goodness as racial segregation is.
2. We keep in mind the impermanence of all human arrangements, reminding ourselves that marriages are as tentative as life itself and that they require adaptation to a future that never stops.
3. We leave room for a few surprises.
4. We can learn to trust the idea that God is glorified by all honest, responsible relationships of love and goodness among people whether they occur as part of marriage or in a life-style a hundred miles from the thought of marriage.

Some social dilemmas of singleness *are* different. A happy single learns to develop new coping skills if he or she has previously been married, especially if children are involved.

But marriage calls for a whole shopping bag full of skills, too—patience, the subordination of personal goals to that which serves the interests of the larger unit, and evolving identities.

Michael Novak in "The Family out of Favor" has written:

People say of marriage that it is boring, when what they mean is that it terrifies them: too many and too deep are its searing revelations, its angers, its rages, its hates, and its loves. They say of marriage that it is deadening, when what they mean is that it drives us beyond adolescent fantasies and romantic dreams. They say of children that they are . . . brats, snots, when what they mean is that the importance of parents with respect to the future of . . . children is now known with greater clarity and exactitude than ever before.

He continues:

I do not want to be disturbed, challenged, troubled. Huge regions of myself belong only to me. Seeing myself through the unblinking eyes of an intelligent, honest spouse is humiliating. Trying to act fairly to children, each of whom is temperamentally different from myself and from each other is baffling. My family bonds hold me back from many opportunities. And yet these bonds are, I know, my liberation. They force me to be a different sort of human being in a way I want and need.

So life asks us to weather various sorts of storms, to look for rainbows overhead whether we are single trying to work out our finances, deciding what the children deserve in the way of parenting and what our own emotional and sexual needs are—doing that without the reassuring presence and share-the-load assistance of another—or trying to grow along with a marriage in such a way that it is not a prison but a mutual adventure.

Somewhere in the vicinity of the "bottom line" are the things that are the same: self-worth, faith in God,

Singleness and Marriage—A Double Celebration

courage, humility, character, bravery, and, most of all, love.

Life's changes grab us and we bobble along on the current attempting to adapt, to learn from yesterday so that we can do better tomorrow. But what does not change is the love that is common to all human experience—married or single—to all stages of the journey.

Marriage is no guarantee of happiness, and singleness is no guarantee of freedom.

They can both be façades that obscure persons behind them. And if the masks fall and the labels are disregarded, then what is there—emptiness or fullness—that is what matters both to God and, ultimately, to ourselves.

God calls us to be children of light and agents of a dream. That is why we pray—to get the blinds drawn back and the windows thrown open so that we can find out who we are. Having found that out, we can then accept either singleness or marriage as a temporary framework both for personal satisfaction and for discovering some transcendent meaning for our hurrying years.

When Mother Teresa of Calcutta was asked what individuals might do to help make this world a better place in which to live, she answered quietly, "Go home and love your families."

That probably surprises us a little. It would not have surprised us if she had said, "Go out and do something to help the poor, or the sick, or the walking wounded—the need is so great." She was not overlooking that side of what it means to obey God. But loving needs a center. We can't change the world without changing our own souls, and only when we are liberated and cleansed and renewed by God's love can we love that part of the world that may not be ready to love us back.

In the final scene of the film version of Charles and Lady Diana's wedding, when the happy couple is driven out of the gate into a crowd-lined street, a benediction is heard in the background against exultant music, uttered, I suppose, by the Archbishop of Canterbury. He is either saying a prayer written for the occasion, or reading from a form of the Anglican liturgy used only for royal moments. One line sounded something like this: "Go out now as kings and queens of love, showing forth in all you do and all that you become the majesty of that love that came to us in Jesus, Lord of all things."

That St. Paul's ceremony was lovely to see, but it did not change the basic assignment, because, whether we are single or married, we are summoned to be light to the world, to be those whom God is counting on to win out and over the darkness.

Jesus said, "Love one another as I have loved you" (John 15:12).

Fulfilling that commandment doesn't demand a ring. It belongs to widows and widowers as much as to newlyweds, to the newly divorced, or never married as much as to the couple celebrating fifty years of marriage. It belongs to women, and it belongs to men.

What it requires is that we forget old stereotypes about both marriage and singleness and get on with the creation of a new order of relationships that suggest the beginning of a new era of our social history.

The first Easter was a long time ago. Yet the whiff of its story, the wonder of its announcement that Christ has come to transform the quality of all our human interactions, lingers on and makes our days more royal romances than footnotes of fate.

Love at Any Age

My eighties are passionate. Old people are not protected from life by engagements, or pleasures, or duties; we are open to our own sentience. When I am with other people I try to find them, or try to make a point in myself from which to make a bridge to them, or I walk on the egg-shells of affection trying not to hurt or misjudge. All this is very tiring, but love at any age takes everything you've got.

—Florida Scott Maxwell, *The Measure of My Days*

Every once in a while a book is published that deserves to be called a blockbuster. It takes the country by storm.

In Civil War days, *Uncle Tom's Cabin* by Harriet Beecher Stowe was that kind of book. More than a book, it was part of the actual shaping of American history. It would make an interesting exercise to go back over the past hundred years and single out those half-dozen books that swayed the world the most. Someone either found something genuinely new to say, something old to say with startling freshness, some taboo to violate, or some message to strike a major chord of the human heart to which millions of people said: "That's the way I feel," or "That's right!" or "Let's do something about this!"

One such writing is called *Passages* by Gail Sheehy. It first appeared in May of 1976 and by March of 1977, nine months later, it had already been through

Love at Any Age

fifteen separate printings! That's literary success written in tall letters.

What made *Passages* so important? Why did it soar to the top of the best-seller lists and stay there for so long?

What it was saying was this: adulthood is not just an assortment of accidental or incidental happenings. Adulthood is a journey, and there is much that is known and predictable about what we may expect as we move through different ages and stages of our adult years.

We haven't always thought that, or been conscious of that. Dr. Benjamin Spock taught us the kinds of things to look for and foster in the development of a new baby. We created mountains of research and are still creating them, on the subject of early childhood development. We have studied adolescence, the formative years. But then, with rare exceptions, we have tended to drop the subject and assume that, now that one is grown, fate takes over. We have known that life will change, but have generally taken the position, for the most part, that those changes will be rather haphazard, the "cookie-crumbles" explanation.

We knew that there is such a thing as middle age (or to use the more "mod" term "middlessence"), that, somewhere along the road we could expect to grow a little pauncher and a little wiser, experience something called menopause, and eventually meet the end of our earthly life. But adult development was not, and probably still is not, taken very seriously.

Yet we have had to begin to take it seriously because people now live longer. They don't have to work as hard, so their bodies are not worn at age fifty. Yet the rate of change—all manners of change—has speeded up, so the truth is that now we end up living not just one life, but several. There has been a revolution in our thinking about women and marriage. We have lived through revolutions in technology, in nutrition, in travel, and in education. These have created a different world—one that has intensified the need to understand more. We need to understand not just the singular passage from youth to age, but also to know as much as we can about all sorts of changes and turns in the road that social scientists are beginning to map out and help us prepare for.

The Book of Hebrews calls Jesus the pioneer of a new order of humanity. Throughout the New Testament, we see him helping people discover what is missing from their lives and redressing the balances.

God is interested in how we respond to the new kind of world and society that we have just been discussing, how we exercise a responsible stewardship of all these possibilities that go along with a growing that never ceases.

In *Passages,* Gail Sheehy talks about something she calls concomitant growth. And, while that sounds like fancy theory, it is not overly difficult to understand, and, for those who have freshly moved into some phase of their journey of adulthood, there is something in that discussion for them.

It is Sheehy's belief that adults are challenged to grow simultaneously in three ways or three areas of their human experience. One is in terms of their vocations, their life work. We want to find a place of usefulness and value, to become good, if we can, at whatever it is we are doing. This used to be particularly true for men. But now it is true for women as well. Part of our ego is wrapped up in some form of vocational achievement. We want to be a good craftsperson or manager or doctor or teacher or builder or baker or candlestick maker. Not all of our identity is bound up with our careers, but some of it is. We yearn to do something significant.

A second area involves relationships with people who come to matter in our lives. We relate, of course, first to the members of our own families, to our parents, our spouses, and to our friends, to teachers, to employers, to our children. And through these encounters we do a considerable amount of growing and changing. Marriages have evolving careers and seasons of their own.

Perhaps it is more accurate to say that we try to relate to one another, but that sometimes these tries misfire and we get too busy to allow them to happen. Even within families, sometimes people don't get to know one another at all. But it's a crucial part of our life story and involves its own kind of adult growing pains as, for example, when our children become adults, and we, who are parents, must learn to let go of them and begin to know them, not just as our offspring but as peers and friends.

A third area of change involves the "Inward Journey," what Maslow calls "self-actualization," the emergence of the self, the you that makes you, you. The life of the soul. Our concern with ultimate realities.

Some of the biggest surprises that go along with movement through the passages of adult development come because one of these three areas, after weeks, or months, or years of neglect, suddenly starts to become awfully important. We try to right our lives, which resemble a boat that starts to tip one way, by shifting our weight to the other side.

That's why the *Passages* writer speaks of concomitant growth, the need to keep alert to changes and growth in all three of those areas of living.

John Claypool, a Southern Baptist minister, describes how males often find the first part of their adult years consumed with getting ahead in their jobs, becoming workaholic—a word we've all gotten to know. Then, he says, men may discover that because of this preoccupation they've lost all touch with other members of their families. Or they've lost touch with their inner selves. Then perhaps as the result of some crisis, a heart attack or divorce, it becomes excruciatingly clear that one of these three areas isn't the whole sum and substance of life, or of happiness. To be a big shot in the company isn't as totally satisfying and need-fulfilling as it looked like it might be. Then there is a great hurrying to make up lost ground, to rediscover one's children, or God, or one's larger self.

Only to find, possibly, that other members of the family are involved in some adjustments of their own.

"Imagine," says Claypool, "the frustration that will develop when one day a man who never gets home before eight suddenly appears at five-thirty with an amorous look on his face and the proposal for a candlelight evening out. Instead, he finds a note on the breakfast room table saying 'Hi! I've decided to take a course at the Community College. There is a TV dinner in the freezer. Don't wait up. I will see you in the morning.' Just think of the social dynamite," he says, "if those involved do not understand what is happening. The man is moving out of a workaholic over-investment to people and to inwardness at the very moment his wife is moving out of an excessive preoccupation with relationships into a desire to become more effective in the marketplace, and not to be aware of this may be disastrous. We need to realize," he says, "that the human psyche has a balancing mechanism at its heart. It is always reaching out in the direction of the underdeveloped, and that must be taken into account."

It is silly to imagine that by knowing enough and planning well we can free our adult lives of stress and mistakes and imbalances. That will never happen. But what faith can do is to help us see life as a whole, to meet it in terms of its total possibilities, and not forfeit the vision that includes our work, our neighbors and friends, and our inward self.

In Alan Alda's movie *Four Seasons* we see a group of adults who like to do things together, but wind up with a whole bunch of conflicts—some comical, some deeply serious—that have to be faced. The movie's message is one we can hardly miss: if we want good and close friends, and if we want to enjoy and keep those friends, we must learn to put up with a lot of crazy and irrational behavior. The other choice is to go our way without them—impoverished and alone.

Age sixty has become an interesting stage of life for me, that marker having recently turned up on my speedometer of years. I have learned that both of the following things are true: our experience as lovers changes as we grow older, and our experience of loving and being loved does *not* change. We need love when we are five and when we are seventy-five. Love's power does not change, and love's permanence does not change. When, as a pastor, I am trying to comfort people or families who are grieving I always try to find an honest way to say that love is eternal, and while we may have to give up the physical presence, the footfalls and smiles of someone who is taken from us by death, at the same time we do not have to give up love. Love is imperishable, greater than death.

David was thirty when he became king. Thirty is

the minimum age specified in the U.S. Constitution for becoming a United States senator. Yes, thirty is a special age.

But so is forty. A magazine article ooh-ed and aah-ed over the fact that both Pete Rose and Carl Yastrzemski were still championship baseball players turning in topnotch performances in almost every game, and both—can you believe this?—*both* have passed their fortieth birthday! If we think back—not so far—but a little way, we may remember what a literary splash Walker Pitkin made with his book *Life Begins at Forty*. Pitkin hit the market with the assumption that such an idea, that life could take on wonderful, new compelling, and valuable meanings—could know some of its best hours of all—after age forty, was surprising and newsworthy.

Of this crisis decade, Gail Sheehy wrote in *Passages* (E. P. Dutton & Co., 1976): "Every one of us can expect a distortion in our sense of time. We have stumbled onto that apostrophe in time between the end of growing up and the beginning of growing old." Maybe so, but growing old is something that actually begins a few minutes after birth.

How about fifty?

That's a nice round number. Fifty is OK. And I treasure the two following statements concerning the attainment of the half-century mark. First, that by the time a person is fifty, he "is responsible for his own face." A way of saying, I suppose, that faces reflect inner philosophies, and that fifty years is enough

Accept No Imitations

time to decide on whether one is going to be a loving, outgoing, positive person, or a jaded and cranky, critical old curmudgeon.

The second is Adlai Stevenson's words referring to the wisdom a person of fifty has that someone twenty does not. In an address he made at Princeton University he called it

> not the knowledge of formulas but of people, places, action. A knowledge not gained by words but by touch, sight, sounds, victories, failures, sleeplessness, devotion, love, the human experiences and emotions of this earth, and perhaps, too, a little faith and little reverence for the things you cannot see. That reverence for the things you cannot see, comes hard and often with pain. It comes when life knocks you down like an express train and just keeps dragging you after it like a slow freight, when the gaiety is crushed out of you and you just feel there's nothing worth waiting for, and so maybe, maybe you try waiting for the Lord.

Then comes sixty. Now, there are new trapeze bars or brass rings to reach out and try to grab.

At sixty we start getting some new kinds of mail, some slightly embarrassing discounts, and questions from friends about future plans. Life also begins to assume some new texture—yes, I think that's the right word: *texture*. We find ourselves stopping to listen to the sounds of living all about us, to listen to a Voice within, and to notice certain truths.

One, that love is a lifelong career and opportunity. Whatever else may be denied us as we make these crossovers into new countries of experience, love is not denied. Whatever we may have to give up, it is not love.

As J. B. Phillips translates, love is "the one thing that still stands when all else has fallen" (I Cor. 13:8).

Sigmund Freud counsels us that we should learn to love deeply and hate wisely. If we're ever going to learn that, we will have learned it by the beginning of the sixth decade, the "inn of the sixth happiness."

Love at sixty suggests a further truth: that we know more *about* love—not simply as a way of looking back and remembering "the way we were," but also as a way of looking up and looking around us. We are more experienced in loving, less anxious to defend our own psychological turf. We have more to give. We know now that love isn't just a spontaneous whiplash; it is something deliberate.

When Dr. Scott Peck writes about the "work" of love, or the courage of love, or when Frederick Speakman comes at us with a book entitled *Love Is Something You Do* we know what these people are talking about. We know love is not emotional flip-flopping, but is commitment, decision, brave and durable, increasingly rugged as it meets test after test and, in the words of the text, never gives up!

At sixty we also speak our love more easily and express it without fear. We speak it faster, too. We don't hold it back. We know love is not the sunlight.

We also find ourselves mixed up in other kinds of love affairs with books, the ocean, astronomy, children, music, travel, flowers and gardening, politics, the Bible, and the great questions the Bible is forever talking about.

We are even ready to love ourselves because we've looked around and decided there aren't any perfect folk we know, so if we love them and enjoy them, why not also love ourselves and applaud our own self-worth?

Love is a four-sided square. We need to love ourselves—to love God, to love others, including those who strike us as strange, different, or even unlovable. And we need to love life.

Life is a sacred tour more than a marathon dance contest.

Frederick Buechner, whose writings are so beautiful and so true to the human heart, has two books that relate his own life story. In them, he ponders the meaning of a disorganized childhood, his father's suicide, his decision to drop out of school, his love of words and books, and his unshakable feeling that faith always has been and always will be the most important word we have. In *The Sacred Journey* (Harper & Row, 1982) he says:

> Deep within history, as it gets itself written down in history books and newspapers, in the letters we write and in the diaries we keep, is sacred history, is God's purpose working itself out in the apparent purposelessness of human history and of our separate histories, is the history, in short of the saving and losing of souls including our own.
>
> A child is born. A friend is lost or found. Out of nowhere

Love at Any Age

comes a sense of peace of foreboding. We are awakened by a dream. Out of the shadowy street comes a cry for help. We must learn to listen to the cock crows and hammering and tick-tock of our lives for the holy and elusive word that is spoken to us out of their depths.

A movie smash in 1982 was *E.T.*, the film story of a little extraterrestrial creature accidentally left behind when a space vehicle that has landed on earth is forced to leave very quickly. He is odd-looking to say the least, but a little boy, Elliott, is determined to get acquainted and to communicate. Elliott and E.T. wind up loving each other, while a lot of other people are frightened and threatened and ready to call out the army and the Detoxification Units.

At one point in the picture when E. T. lies ill and near death, a physician-scientist looking down on the pitiful little form, then across at tearful Elliott, says to Elliott: "I'm glad he met *you* first."

We meet love. We experience love, enjoy love, and participate in love by participating in one another's lives—in one another's yearnings and needs and tragedies and struggle to become, for in them, and in all those experiences we see and feel ourselves and we are comforted for we know that we are not alone.

I like to speak about the love that will not let us go, that will not let us down, and will not let us off.

And I like the experience of sixty. Is it the equal of twenty? Oh, yes. Is it a good time of life? Oh, yes, it is a good time. Is our happiness and success in living dependent upon what happens or doesn't happen to us, or what we do with what happens or doesn't happen? The latter of course. We are made in the image of God. And we are made to love. Love lights up our life. Writes Paul: "Leave no claim outstanding against you, except that of mutual love" (Rom. 13:8 NEB).

If God has so loved us in Christ, then we also are without choice. We must also love one another.

A few years ago I compiled this personal list of that which both guides us through change, yet remains beyond change's power:

Life without God is incomplete.

Worship, prayer, and giving are part of the process of growing into the likeness of Christ and toward a knowledge of God's will and purpose for us.

Communicating with persons of all ages, from the youngest to the oldest, and acknowledging that they are made in the image of God is the best gift anyone can either give or receive.

All that is dehumanizing in life—ignorance, war, sexism or racism, self-righteousness or hate—is to be resisted.

Life is made both more exciting and significant by exposure to beauty—the beauty of music, flowers, stained glass, and faces.

When we are called to grieve, we do not have to grieve alone, and no one need perish of loneliness.

We are part of a larger community of values, and the needs of that larger group must be treated as conscientiously as our own.

We have a continuing word to speak about freedom—

freedom from fear, from emptiness and aimlessness of living, from sin, from ourselves.

Faith, hope, and love are life's sovereign centers. In the end they prove invincible.

James W. Angell

That still sounds pretty good—like some of Cartagena's best.

Life Is a Ten-Foot Wall

For by You I can run against a troop,
And by my God I can leap over a wall.

—Psalm 18:29 NKJV

To be the best in the world is quite a star to have shining in your personal sky. Indeed, the symbol of the 1984 Olympic games is a star in motion.

The opening processional—the flags, the torch, the link with yesterday, the at-least-for-this-moment transcendence of the local and the parochial in the name of all humanity moves us to a sense of solemn pride. The anthems, the medals, the countries, the languages, the perfection.

But, of course, the Olympics are no more immaculate than life is. We cannot and do not know absolute perfection this side of heaven or we would become gods of our own.

Who can forget the tragedy of twelve years ago when five or six Israeli athletes were killed for political reasons, just as the games were getting underway? Out of that awful news story this poem came to me:

Life Is a Ten-Foot Wall

> The whole world is Munich
> All men are Jews
> Civilization is weeping
> In barracks 31.
>
> Bicycle racing
> Runners gaining
> Vaulters vaulting
> Discuses spinning;
> Volleyball players spiking;
> Wrestlers straining;
> Gold medals shining;
>
> But the jungle winning.
>
> James W. Angell

There is, of course, more than one form of excellence, but the excellence of love set forth unforgettably in Jesus Christ, remains the highest achievement any of us can know. That is the theme of all four Gospels.

But take a look also at Psalm 18, a song of deliverance ascribed to David who, following escape from the hands of Saul's soldiers, said or sang:

> For You will light my lamp;
> The Lord my God will enlighten my darkness.
> For by You I can run against a troop,
> And by my God I can leap over a wall.
> (Ps. 18:28-29 NKJV)

If you have a long memory, you might remember that those words were once used by an ex-nun who left the convent, then wrote her own life story with the title *I Leap over a Wall.*

I have another example in mind, though, as we think about leaping—not over monastic enclosures, or over high and low hurdles, or over the high jump bar, or over that eighteen-foot wooden or plastic mountain known as the pole vault, but over barriers that limit us and challenge us to what the Bible calls steadfastness, as endurance. Let your attention land for a second in one of those final paragraphs of the Book of Revelation. "He that overcometh shall inherit all things; and I will be his God, and he shall be my son" (Rev. 21:7 KJV).

How, though, could we have any real discussion about walls without Robert Frost?

> Something there is that doesn't love a wall,
> That wants it down.

The Berlin Wall, too, cannot be forgotten or ignored. Somehow, someway, it must come down in our lifetime. "Something there is" that hates a wall like that and all the costly alienation it signifies.

The Great Wall of China we were told was the only man-made creation that astronauts could recognize from space in those early flights, though I believe I remember reading that the lights of New York City ran a close second.

And the Old Testament is full of stories about walls—the walls of Jericho, the walls of Jerusalem, those old early securities against the foe which are no more, though the wailing wall is still there.

Remnants of the old Roman walls can still be seen as you drive through rural England. The castle and town walls of medieval Europe offered protection and safety from all kinds of perils. They are now replaced by our own 1983 walled-in communities grandly advertised in the real estate section of *The Times*—protection at a price from the ugly and the criminal.

But those are not the toughest walls people have to deal with.

The walls of fear, the walls of loneliness and jealousy, ignorance, cold silence, and secular selfishness are thicker and more difficult to penetrate or topple.

Yet we read of One who has "broken down the dividing wall of hostility, . . . that he might create . . . one new man in the place of the two, so making peace" (Eph. 2:14-15).

At home, a favorite TV program has long been "One Day at a Time." And, while all the actors on that show are among the best, Bonnie Franklin as Ann Romano shines with a special human light.

In one segment, eight or ten months ago, things have reached their latest crisis moment in that single-parent household when Bonnie turns on the family and confronts them with some homespun philosophy out of her childhood. Using those familiar flashes of bright, strawberry blonde emotion, she said her dad once told her that life is a ten-foot wall, and the sooner she found that out, the better off she would be. She said he brought her up to believe there is a way over that wall. Not around it. Over it. And that she'd never stopped thinking she could do it.

In Scott Peck's *The Road Less Traveled* (Simon & Schuster, 1978) we encounter another honest reminder of this same life-principle:

> Life is difficult.
> This is a great truth, one of the greatest truths. It is a great truth because once we truly see this truth, we transcend it. . . . Because once it is accepted, the fact that life is difficult no longer matters.

He goes on in that valuable book of his to say:

> Most people do not fully see this truth that life is difficult. Instead they moan more or less incessantly, noisily or subtly, about the enormity of their problems, their burdens, and their difficulties as if life were generally easy, as if life *should* be easy. I know about this moaning . . . because I have done my share.

It is, he insists, problem solving that gives life its meaning and glory, its high significance. And he quotes another Franklin, first name, Benjamin: "Those things that hurt, instruct" and Carl Jung: "Neurosis is always a substitute for legitimate suffering." Then he accuses us, in love, by saying that most of us "to a greater or lesser degree attempt to

Life Is a Ten-Foot Wall

avoid problems. We procrastinate, hoping that they will go away. We ignore them, forget them, pretend they do not exist. We even take drugs to assist us in ignoring them."

Dr. Peck lays out on the table, for us to look at, four tools of discipline with which to deal constructively with suffering and difficulty: the delay of gratification, acceptance of responsibility, a dedication to truth, and what he calls balancing—mastering the art of living in both present, past, and future but not exclusively in any one of those temporal dimensions and living for ourselves and for and on behalf of others, but not exclusively for either.

Life is a ten-foot wall.

But with others pushing up from below, and ourselves delivered from self-pity or illusion that life is something other than what it really is, we will make it to the other side.

One wall all of us gain experience in trying to surmount is despair, gray despair, debilitating, energy-sapping despair. Feelings of defeat, uselessness, and failure—of the death even of our own anger, to say nothing of the death of our dreams. Depression, which is, in most cases an unresolved state of sadness or sorrow.

That is a wall. Not a crannied wall with a flower in it. Rather, one of imprisonment and bondage. The opposite spiritual pole of excellence and joy, of feeling fulfilled, glad to be ourselves and alive in this world at this time.

But there's a way over the wall of ourselves. And, if we can find it, we may also be able to help hungry persons learn where to find bread.

I won't pose as an expert on depression. I am not. But I've been in and out of despair, like you have, and I know that more often than not it is caused by exaggerated dependency. My family has let me down. The congregation has let me down. God has let me down. I have lost some precious source of love. My profession or my health has let me down. Someone whom I needed, has died, and they shouldn't have done that. Selfness is diminished and we feel sad because we are less than we were or think we have the right to be. A wall is rising. It needs to be kicked apart.

There are at least a hundred titles in every bookstore on the subject of self-worth and probably most of them filled with pretty fair first-aid advice.

Spencer Marsh says he tries to keep his own soul fit by trying to invent at least one mini-adventure experience each week, and at least one maxi-adventure every year. I've tried to model on that scheme with such simple techniques in the "mini category" as:

- buying a new book or necktie
- seeing a new movie or play
- visiting an art museum or going to a concert
- writing a letter to some one I haven't seen in years

Life Is a Ten-Foot Wall

- making a new friend
- going out to dinner or planning a party
- getting out of town
- creating a poem
- playing in a golf tournament
- thinking how exciting it would be to take flying lessons
- attending a lecture
- noticing a sunset, poring over an atlas, or a boat ride, or train ride, or walk on the beach

All of these are options that require initiative on my part to make them happen. They represent ways of helping me stay in love with life and maybe also in love with myself.

Maxi-adventures? Well, that list is necessarily shorter, but it could include:

- a cross-country trip or visit to Paris or Australia
- enrollment for advanced study at a university
- relocation, the beginning of a new job
- the writing of a book, the completion of a painting the fulfillment of some long-standing dream

It would be shallow to imagine that all we are talking about here are lists of recreational possibilities, because life's deepest adventures frequently arise out of other sorts of experiences—things like heart attacks, divorces, the death of someone extremely close to us, or some other radical development that forces us into new territories of growth.

Lewis Thomas says that because the unit of all life, the DNA molecule, was ordained from the beginning to make little mistakes, evolution is possible—evolution from lower to higher forms of life. This idea of error is revealing, says Thomas, "because it comes from a root word meaning to wander about looking for something."

Dr. Theodore Loder commented on this in a sermon:

> Let us [never] fear to wander about looking for something—something new, new ways to do things, new ways to be together. . . . Let us look for something in each other, something graceful, something needing release, something aching to be given, a talent to be risked, something to be praised and enjoyed, together. Let us look for something healing in and among us. Let us look for mercy in each and all of us. Let us wander about looking for, looking to be a colony of heaven.

So here is a wall to watch—one that is made out of our own unsure feelings, self-doubt and limited horizons. Maybe, too, of the crumbly illusion that God has decided to kick us around a bit and doesn't care what happens to us.

Another is one that grows up between people and nations because of differences that wind up looking like threats instead of opportunities. Walls of fear and mistrust. Sin and de-humanity. They keep people apart and are made of lies and half-truths and an arms race.

They rest on foundations of paranoia and, our old pal, self-doubt again—insecurity about our own beauty and worth and right to be here. Half the pain of the world is the result of people forgetting who they are. So they, we, wind up defensive and blind to one of the world's most attractive ideas: different is beautiful.

In Claremont we couldn't think of letting a year go by without hearing the children's choir sing at least once those marvelous lines of Richard Avery and Donald Marsh:

> Diff'rent is beautiful! God bless variety!
> Just look around and see:
> Diff'rent is beautiful! Beautiful!
>
> If all girls were housewives,
> How awful that would be.
> If all boys were maitre d's,
> How dull & boring.
> Can't you see that God made the housewife and maitre d',
> God in his liberality!
> Doctor and lawyer and Indian Chief,
> Banker and someone who needs relief,
> Garbage collector and TV star,
> Student and teacher and what you are.
>
> Just look around and see:
> Diff'rent is beautiful! Beautiful!

And how about those Special Olympics that feature the remarkable potential of those who have problems of physical disability yet who hold in common all the same needs, sometimes even taller talents than the able-bodied?

A couple of miles from where I live and work is a rehabilitation hospital named Casa Colina. One of the patients there is a young man named Mike Smith, a victim of a crash in a crop-dusting helicopter when its rotors became tangled in a high tension wire that was invisible in the bright desert sunshine. He has become a champion wheelchair racer, finishing the Boston Marathon in 2 hours and 42 minutes. His is gallantry of the highest order.

How about the wall, too, or is it a river, that separates the world that is from the world that is yet to be, that divides today and tomorrow, the known from the unknown, life from death?

At funeral services, ministers are accustomed to saying death is not a wall but a door, that the rose finds its way through the crevice and unfolds itself on the other side.

But those who mourn need more than poetry and more than the testimonies of the near dying who report seeing a very bright light. They need more than science. More than solace and reassurance. They need hope—hope that is muscular, that can stand the test of the fire, hope born of their own faith history, confirmed by life in community made credible to their hearts because God has become credible, real—because in the Risen Christ they have come to know the God who will not let them go, will not let them down, and will not let them off.

Because death has such finality to it, the quality of the irretrievable, it is a wall. Let's not kid ourselves out of that. Christian faith is not one based on a theory of immortality, though Paul uses the word. Rather, it is based upon resurrection, a wild leap into a new world, the staking out of a new life, new beginnings and new adventures. We are not death-deniers. We are life-celebrators—life in all its fabulous dimensions here but that also outlasts, outreaches, outdreams all earth can offer.

The Athletes and the Rules

> ANAHEIM (AP)—*Prominent Southern Californians and people from 14 other states and six other nations are victims of a $500 million-a-year swindle using overvalued gems to buy property, police say.*
>
> *"This is the largest such fraud ever detected in California," police spokesman Dean Gross said Wednesday. "In the last couple of months, every time we turn a page in the investigation the whole thing has just mushroomed."*
>
> *The victims included "several prominent Southern Californians," Gross said. "One was a major Los Angeles athlete, but we have agreed not to release his name."*
>
> —Pomona, *Progress Bulletin*

Not everyone reads the sports pages, or knows or cares about "I" formations, earned run averages, or the full-court press. Still, athletic competition is such an emotional and pervasive part of American life that there is no way to understand our national history or spirit without taking these phenomena into account.

Our games are our entertainment, intended as showcases of excellence. Excellence is on everybody's agenda these days, including those concerned with public education who seek to turn back what one investigative commission referred to as a "rising tide of mediocrity," and spoke of the United States as a nation "at risk" because our educational systems appear so lacking. Professional sports, though, seem to have their interest in that subject rather befogged by salary battles, drug arrests, and lawsuits.

I was never a very good athlete. I wanted to be, and I gave my best out on the football field earning two

The Athletes and the Rules

letters, and once played catcher on an American Legion baseball team. But what I lacked in eye-hand coordination and natural speed and quickness couldn't be made up for by burning desire. I learned to play golf, though, and I try to avoid church meetings on Monday nights to watch NFL football.

The concern with excellence raises a question for me, What is the connection between the passion to excel—to be the best, the swiftest, the most graceful, the finest in the world—and the exhortation of Jesus to "be perfect"—the call of God to make our own lives outstanding assets in the kingdom of his purpose?

How, though, can you think or talk about the total excellence of human beings unless you also deal with the heart, the spirit, the will—with ethics, and a relationship with God? Excellence isn't really excellence unless it is also realized as faith, hope, love, commitment, and social righteousness.

The Olympics have a long, interesting history, stretching back to at least the year 776 B.C., when the Greeks began compiling a list of victors. It was the beauty of Greek athletes that gave birth to the art of sculpture—maybe even to history itself. At least it is these records of winners that seem to mark the beginning of dated history. Yet, it is the birth of a Child that dates history in another way, that has given rise to the art of other kinds of achievement.

When, at age twenty-two, I left for the military as World War II began, my church gave me a New Testament. A note in the flyleaf asked me to notice

Accept No Imitations

especially the lines from I Timothy that speak of the good soldier of Jesus Christ, the hard-working farmer, and the athlete—all called to accountability for giving a good performance.

The desire to win can, I suppose, be largely a matter of ego, of hunger for recognition. And there is nothing wrong with confessing that.

Peter Marshall is supposed to have burst into the house at five o'clock one evening, soon after he had taken over as chaplain of the United States Senate, saying "Catherine! Senator Vandenberg called me Peter today!"

We enjoy recognition and applause, winning championships, the idea that the world, or some little piece of the world, will remember us or what we did, the thought of being someone else's hero or model. And, if we cannot be Mark Spitz or Bruce Jenner or Peggy Fleming or Nadia Comaneci, we can enjoy that same winning feeling if Texas beats Oklahoma, or UCLA beats USC, almost as much as if we had carried the ball over the goal line ourselves.

But what is meant by that New Testament sentence "An athlete is not crowned unless he competes according to the rules" (II Tim. 2:5)? Is Christianity a religion of rules—or something else?

The easy way, perhaps the only accurate way to deal with the question is to answer "grace." We are the covenant people of grace. We believe that there is no satisfactory answer to our sin and failure and

The Athletes and the Rules

imperfection *except* God's grace. "In my hands no price I bring; / Simply to thy cross I cling."

Many if not most services of worship conclude with words that sound something like this: "The *grace* of the Lord Jesus Christ be with us all."

But grace doesn't rule out effort.

It is said of the Puritans concerning their belief in predestination that the more they believed it the harder they worked to make sure that they were the chosen of God. The more fervently we believe that our hope is in the forgiving love of God, not in ourselves, the more eagerness I believe we have to move out to show the world who we are and to join God in rescuing it from hate and despair, from shoddiness and indifference.

Few things make any bigger difference in the sort of life we live and the ways we treat other people than the way we feel about ourselves. It is almost impossible to affirm life and those around us if we are tied up in knots by self-denial or by feeling unbeautiful and unnecessary.

But self-esteem is more than saying yes to ourselves *as* we are. It also represents some kind of self-authenticated view about what we feel we would like to become.

Jesus Christ is the Lord of excellence who enables us both to feel accepted of God, free in that acceptance, and, at the same time, dissatisfied to stay where we are.

In the play *Waiting for Godot* there's a conversation

Accept No Imitations

in which Estragon, one of the characters, takes off his boots and leaves them as a gift for whoever might come along and need them. Vladimir asks him if he is comparing himself to Jesus. Estragon answers, "I've been comparing myself to him all my life."

As for Jesus, surely it would not be fair to say he lived his life without rules even though he was not afraid to break rules which to him had become pious substitutes for genuine compassion and sincere behavior.

"And he came to Nazareth, where he had been brought up; and he went to the synagogue, as his custom was, on the sabbath day. And he stood up to read" (Luke 4:16).

It may be that we shouldn't call that a rule, but it was a habit of his life. As was prayer and fasting. He knew the Ten Commandments and honored them. He was not without structure and discipline, yet he saw rules as false limits upon larger possibilities people are capable of—greater love and larger living. His enemy was not the law; it was mediocrity and phony pride.

Excellence, yes. But something else to which we also say yes. To the broken side of life for those to whom the love of excellence is a lost dream, a forgotten wonder, something so far out of reach that one no longer feels its magnetic draw.

An evangelist speaking in a rescue mission one night brought his appeal to a dramatic climax by reciting the words of the famous Kipling poem "If."

The Athletes and the Rules

You will remember how it ends:

If you can fill the unforgiving minute
With sixty seconds' worth of distance run,
Yours is the Earth and everything that's in it,
And—which is more—you'll be a Man, my son!

A hand went up in the back of the room and with it came a question, "But what if you can't?"

The answer is that, yes, we need a Christ in our lives, a model of excellence, stars to hitch our wagons to, to know and to believe that we are fashioned for greatness and goodness—even for perfection. But we also need to know that when we fall short of all those good and glorious ambitions God has given us, when we fail in ways large and small, God remains there to affirm us as individuals of worth and to love us back to hope and faith in ourselves.

In 1983 the Brooklyn Bridge was one hundred years old. During the centennial celebration people recalled the story of its builder.

John Roebling was born in Germany and came to western Pennsylvania in 1831 where he started the first factory in America to manufacture wire rope. He dreamed of building a suspension bridge over the East River connecting Brooklyn and New York. Accomplishing his dream took fourteen years. The work had to be carried on in the face of danger, ridicule, setbacks, and even the breakdown of his health as a result of weeks and weeks spent in compressed air chambers under the surface of the river. After that the only way he could continue to oversee the work was from his apartment overlooking the construction site—giving orders through his son, Washington, then just thirty-two years old, and his wife, Emily. But the result, though it doesn't affect us that way any longer, was in 1883 one of the artistic and engineering marvels of the early part of the Industrial Age. The Brooklyn Bridge with its cables sixteen inches thick, its soaring towers with all stonework hoisted upward a hundred feet by steam, was the patient fulfillment of one man's dreams.

Excellence, then, is recognizable in surgery and ballet, in the forward pass and needlepoint, in the theater and the cultivation of a Peace rose. Haven't we listened to a Beverly Sills or Isaac Stern and said to ourselves, "Oh, to be able to do any single thing on earth that well, that exquisitely!" To run, to dance, to sing, to paint, to fly...

A shipbuilding firm in the East has long had as its motto: "We build good ships, at a profit if we can, at a loss if we must, but always good ships."

The apostle Paul's best-remembered statement concerning excellence is this: "Whatever is true, whatever is honorable, whatever is just, whatever is pure, whatever is lovely, whatever is gracious, if there is any excellence, if there is anything worthy of praise, think about these things" (Phil. 4:8).

He has another statement we ought to look at also. In I Corinthians 12 Paul has developed another of his "Book of Lists" and is running down all the different ways God is served through the church—through gifts of teaching and healing and interpretation and administration and helpfulness, as though trying to sort out all of these in terms of their respective importance.

Finally, he says, "But let me tell you about the most important service of all, the greatest excellence we know anything about." Then he opens the famous chapter 13: "Though I speak with the tongues of men and of angels and have not love . . . I am nothing. Though I am brilliant academically or noble through sacrifice—even if I give away everything I have, or am smart enough to decode the future, but have not love, I am nothing" (author's adaptation).

What he is telling us is that anything we say, or any conclusion we reach about excellence must find its ultimate expression in *love*.

It is in the cross of Christ where the excellence of our successes and the excellence of grace that covers our failures come together and constitute one truth.

God *does* call us to be our best, to strive, to reach, to match the splendor of creation with magnificent inventions of our own.

God's Spirit doesn't show up in our lives only to comfort us. God's Spirit also calls us to make the most of our lives, the most of our years, the most of each opportunity.

To excel means to go beyond an old limit, to transcend what someone once called "the sin of average living." That probably means that the desire to win is partly an ego journey, but it is also partly

Accept No Imitations

God inviting us to set new standards, to move history forward, to take our talents—whether they are one, five, or ten—and glorify life and earth by using them.

But God also shows us another side to life, offering us acceptance into the kingdom—even when we have not lived up to our best, or when we have fallen on our face.

One role the church has is to keep excellence always before us:

> A vision of peace between nations.
> A vision of honesty and integrity in how we
>   live and deal with each other.
> A vision of justice and of concern for
>   the hungry and half-forgotten.
> A vision of moral decency and wholesomeness
>   that isn't X-rated.
> A vision of the Church which, in spite of
>   its faults, is the Body of Christ.
> A vision of America which, in spite of her faults,
>   is dedicated to being and remaining a free,
>   self-governing society and one nation under God.
> A high vision of our own worth as human beings.
> A vision of God.
>
> James W. Angell

We are certainly well-supplied with visions of hell. At our house we often close out the day by watching the late news, with its hurts, bleeding, its freeway accidents, its fires, floods, rough-and-tumble politics, cruelties, bombings, rapes, and robberies. To hide from these is to deny another form of excellence—caring. But neither can we let the eleven o'clock news

The Athletes and the Rules

become for us the only definition we have of the universe.

Paul said, "I will show you a still more excellent way" (I Cor. 12:31*b*).

And that is what the cross says, too. It will not allow cynicism or hate to have the last word. It will not let the crowd shouting, "Crucify, crucify!" be the only definition of the world or the race we have left. Over against that cry is the summons of faith, the love that will not let us go, the forgiveness that will not let us die, the God who will not let us forget who we are.

We bear God's image. If that were the only thing the church has left to say to the world, it would be worth spending everything else we have to keep that from becoming forgotten.

So let us make friends with excellence. With the promise of mercy that makes each day a new beginning, you can believe that what God thinks of you is more crucial than what you think of yourself.

I had the privilege of knowing Thomas Merton and, on two occasions, of spending time alone with him. Merton will be remembered, not only as one of the great poets of modern times, but also as one of those rare souls who seemed to understand more about creative silence and deep prayer than most of us.

In one conversation he said something I will never forget. He may have been quoting someone else—perhaps one of the saints of an age-long past—but his remark was this, "Man is God's trophy." With his

Accept No Imitations

words I caught a glimpse of each of us as God's most interesting idea, most colossal investment and triumph.

Perhaps *we ourselves* are God's vision of excellence. Perhaps that is not only all that we really know. But also all that we need to know.

> You, who ride the thunder,
> Do you know what it is to dream and drudge and throb?
> I wonder.
> Did it come at you with a rush, your dream, your plan?
> If so, I know how you began,
> Yes, with rapt face and sparkling eyes,
> Swinging the hot globe out between the skies, . . .
> And then—
> Men!
> I see it now.
> O God, forgive my pettish row!
> I see your job. While ages crawl
> Your lips take laboring lines, your eyes a sadder light
> For man, the fire and flower and center of it all—
> Man won't come right!
> After your patient centuries,
> Fresh starts, recastings, tired Gethsemanes
> And tense Golgothas, he, your central theme,
> Is just a jangling echo of your dream.
> Grand as the rest may be, he ruins it.
> Why don't you quit?
> Crumple it all and dream again! But no;
> Flaw after flaw, you work it out, revise, refine— . . .
> Dear God, how you must love your job!
> Help me, as I love mine.
>
> Badger Clark, "The Job"

Run for Your Life

The findings from the excellent companies amount to an upbeat message. There is good news from America. Good management practice today is not resident only in Japan. But, more important, the good news comes from treating people decently and asking them to shine, and from producing things that work.

—In Search of Excellence: Lessons
from America's Best Run Companies,
Thomas J. Peters and Robert H.
Watterman, Jr.

The toughest of the Olympic races is the marathon. Though there is no official world's record because the courses vary so much, the best time for the twenty-six miles plus eighty-five yards is a little over two hours, and that was run by Derek Clayton of Australia.

If you remember watching the 1976 Montreal Race on television, you may recall what a dramatic event it was, with a young man by the name of Frank Shorter representing the U.S.

Much of it was run through the rain, through the streets of Montreal, through the neighboring countryside, up hill and down. Darkness came, with the hard distance gradually wearing away the endurance of most of the runners—all of whom had trained for years to pit their strength against the best in the world. With three or five miles left to go, it became obvious that Shorter of America and Waldemar

Cierpinksi of East Germany were ahead and would undoubtedly finish in first and second place.

Shorter was leading to no one's surprise since he had won in 1972. But then Cierpinksi made his move. He pulled up even, then with his eyes intense, his chest thrust against the night wind and rain, he surged out in front of them all.

In the background, the cameras showed the lighted stadium as Cierpinksi circled the big oval toward the finish. The crowd stood and gave him a huge ovation to urge him on. Then came Shorter, and the crowd rose again and cheered another fine athlete. Cierpinksi won. Shorter was just fifty seconds behind.

Among the many marvelous metaphors the Bible uses to help explain God and the meaning of life is the race. The sun mounts the eastern sky like a runner (Ps. 19:6), and that old philosopher-friend, Ecclesiastes, notes that "the race is not to the swift, nor the battle to the strong, nor bread to the wise, nor riches to the intelligent, nor favor to the men of skill; but time and chance happen to them all" (Eccles. 9:11).

And the Christianized Jews to whom the Letter of the Hebrews was written were also addressed as sinners (see Heb. 12:1) but their spiritual energy was beginning to fade. The race was proving to be longer than many had thought. Persecution and suffering were becoming "old stuff," and the glow of the earlier conversion was fading out. Some of us with considerable experience trying to put faith into practice might, I'm sure, echo some of that discouragement. Life isn't all "Chariots of Fire" and Christmas mornings. There are Februarys and Marches and Junes and Septembers. Some tragedies almost knock us out of the apple tree. There are accidents, and illnesses, and family breakups, and hillside stranglers and storms. We do our best to cope—to manage these adverse circumstances. But at some point we have to yield ultimate control of the outcome. We have to rediscover the secret of *release*.

Part of being a Christian is letting go. Football passers have to master the quick release, and we must learn to release our grip on a lot of things, including our material possessions.

What is standing in *your* way to an Olympic life? Is it fear? Guilt? Greed? A bad image of yourself which only you can dismantle and discard? A grudge against a relative? Are you mad at God? Afraid to dare? Afraid of making a mistake, of being laughed at, of being yourself? Those fears deserve to be let go. Open your hand, open your heart—and let them fly away.

Parents must also find a way to release their children. They can guard them, love them, treasure them, but can't take upon their shoulders the outcome of their lives. To try to seize that responsibility is usurpation. It is to deny them something which is their own, even the right to fail.

To carry the burden of an old mistake, too, is like pulling a big swinging, swaying trailer behind us. Is not the beginning of mercy to be merciful to one's self?

Stress is excessive pressure created by worry, overwork, guilt, and fear. It is the unwanted dividend of exceeding our limits, often the result of forgetting we are not gods but the children of God.

The gospel rescues us from these overloads in a variety of ways. It shows a life-purpose that leads us to reject the disproportionate spending of our energies for wealth, fame, and power. It helps us understand that we are already deeply loved by God and that we need not burn ourselves out in a mad search for personal validation elsewhere. And it offers us creative, courageous uses of failed relationships and physical sufferings, helping us turn them from tragedies into occasions of growth.

Emerald-type Christianity makes demands that seem to increase stress, defined as the pain-producing distance between what we are and what we yearn to be. But more than this—far more—is its offer of forgiveness and spiritual freedom.

Prayer, the nourishment that comes by reading the Scriptures, worship in community, service to others, sharing love and faith, all help us be still and know that God is God. These disciplines enable us to take time for beauty and persons, to relax and be borne along by the river instead of angrily thrashing at the waters, wondering whom to blame.

And beyond release lies *renewal*—the reclaiming of our commitment, which turns out to be the opposite of "letting go." If we are called to "let go" of something, we must also *grab hold* of something. We can't live on the food we ate a week ago, or the air we breathed an hour ago. I can't survive on the theological training I received twenty-five years ago. No church can survive on the stewardship of yesterday's members. None of us can take what we were in 1974 and make it do in 1984.

"A dance," said Janet, a dance instructor, "isn't like a painting you can hang on the wall and enjoy over and over. And it's not," she went on, "like a piece of music that can be played over many times. It exists only for a moment; then disappears as fast as it came."

We could argue that a dance might be filmed. We still see, occasionally, an old Ginger Rogers–Fred Astaire, or Gene Kelly film. Still, I like Janet's parable. Life is a ballet, and we have to keep dancing—listening for the changing rhythms of a changing world.

Another spiritual discipline might be to *refer*. Jesus is the reference beyond ourselves whose life seems to ask for reserves of strength we didn't know we had.

I'm not sure what long-distance runners concentrate on as part of the mental mastery that keeps them going, but I am sure they must fix their minds on something that is high and inspiring just as prisoners sustain themselves by thoughts of home.

On the Sunday after Easter, a certain imaginative

Accept No Imitations

Sunday school teacher took some old empty pantyhose containers—those that look like eggs—and gave each of the class members one with the instruction to go outside and look around for something that represented new life.

When the boys and girls returned with the eggs and opened them, one by one, most of the what-you'd-expect items were there: flowers, leaves, a butterfly, a bud from a tree. One, though, contained a rock and the kids laughed. "Who picked a rock?" they asked. "That's not like new life." But the boy who had brought it said, "I chose a rock because I wanted to be different, and being different is part of being new." That sounded like a rather sophisticated argument, but whether the class was convinced or not they let it pass.

A few containers later, another was opened and it was empty. This brought even more scorn and disbelief. The teacher waited to see if anyone would take responsibility for the empty egg. And someone did. A Downs Syndrome youngster about eight said, "It's mine. It's empty because the tomb is empty."

The shepherds went with haste after they heard the angels sing. Peter and John raced each other to the Easter tomb.

> We raced, yes, raced
> To see if it was true.
> Running, running, running:
> Legs pounding,

Run for Your Life

Shoulders straining,
Lungs bursting.
My body was a giant pendulum of faith and doubt,
Arms swinging,
Thoughts alternating:
   He must be dead!
   Perhaps he is alive!
Hopes rising:
   He lives!
Hope diminishing:
   I was there when we buried him.
The trees whipped by my vision
Solid and fixed, like the stone at the tomb.
It is just a tale the women told to soothe their grief.
The wind brushed by my cheek,
Invisible and free, like his love
Whispering of miracles.
But suppose it is true.
Running, running, running.
                       Sue Spencer

In George Sheehan's book, *Running and Being,* he describes what it's like to breakthrough the barrier of one's second and third wind. A runner feels like he or she has reached the end of the road—no reserves at all remain. Then, something happens; the body lets loose its buried secret power, and, says Dr. Sheehan, "Then I know that I am made for more!"

That, for me, is a parable of the resurrection, the ground of a faith position that says it is just as important to believe in the beauty of the future as it is to plan intelligently for it. It is against those dangers which add up to apocalypse now, but is also *for* a kingdom of justice and peace.

Jim Peck described us in these words:

> We are the ones who have torn ourselves away from our Creator and have taken flight. We are the ones who, like sheep, have gone astray, turning each one to his own way. We are the ones who have not tolerated God's Lordship and are now in varying stages of escape. We are the fugitives! We are the vagabonds! We are the Gingerbread People!

We won't always "keep the faith" either individually or corporately. We will have times when running will be irresistible, as problem after problem piles up on our doorstep. But grace will come to us in such moments, to remind us that there are two kinds of running. One says no, the other, yes.

Remember Malcolm Boyd's sparkling prayer?

> It's morning, Jesus. It's morning, and here's that light and sound all over again
>
> I've got to move fast . . . get into the bathroom, wash up, grab a bite to eat, and run some more.
> I just don't feel like it, Lord. What I really want to do is to get back into bed, pull up the covers, and sleep. All I seem to want today is the big sleep, and here I've got to run all over again.
> Where am I running? You know these things I can't understand. It's not that I need to have you tell me. What counts most is just that somebody knows, and it's you. That helps a lot.
> So I'll follow along, okay? But lead, Lord. Now I've got to run. Are you running with me Jesus?

We have a choice. To run like deer—afraid of changes we don't understand, afraid of death, afraid of people different from ourselves, afraid of the world—or, to run shepherd-like toward them, toward tomorrow, toward a better day. One will make us a truant; the other a pioneer.

Raised Arms and Scoreboard Lights

"I only know that summer sang in me a little while,"
wrote Gerard Manley Hopkins, "that sings no more."
Come on, Gerard, that song cannot end
As long as God sends songbirds north,
March rains to make the good earth lush and green.
All things collapse
    eventually, yes,
      Save God. But I've seen summer splashed
All over things in the middle of drifts, and
        hunks of freezing stone.
          If love is there, if there are those who care
            whatever emptiness it is we feel
Then summer's Real, then summer sings,
        the calendar's irrelevant.

        —James W. Angell, in *Slice Me a Piece of Summer*

No matter who we are, or where we live, victories are crucial. Victories in all sizes.

Victories are important for political candidates, baseball pitchers, and nations. They have to do with the diagnosis of cancer and with high school or college graduation.

We stand up and shout, "We're number one!" Or we declare a public holiday, make a "V" with our second and third fingers, or give trophies to one another. Or tell stories to our grandchildren—Moses escapes from Pharaoh at the Red Sea; David slays the nine-foot Philistine giant, Goliath.

The Book of Revelation is filled with battle stories, dragons, angelic fires, and multicolored horses. And one of the favorite words in the book is "hallelujah," affirming the final victory of Jesus Christ over every sort of adversary and over every historical expression of evil.

Raised Arms and Scoreboard Lights

Today the United States is trying to win a victory—a victory over economic recession. Another over an epidemic of drug abuse. Why do so many people use drugs? That must tell us something about the kind of spiritual starvation that exists in people's lives. Even soft drugs of the sleep-ease, aspirin variety develop into chalky crutches. The average daily consumption of Tylenol prior to the scare was thirty million tablets daily.

Another over criminality.

Another over a racism that will not quit.

Another over an arms race. So that the nations of the world can use their capabilities to construct and create things rather than preparing to defend themselves against one another's missilery.

How important such victories are if we are to survive emotionally and feel right and good about ourselves!

Bob, a high school student, failed a couple of courses and began to be down on himself. Then he made the football team and, in his senior year, made the all-star team. The heart came back into him when that happened. Young people need victories to help them believe in themselves. All of us need victories. Love is a victory, sometimes a victory at sea.

I belong to the World War II generation who remember totally blacked out nights on ships, weeks spent in convoys crossing the Atlantic or defending our nation's interests in the Mediterranean, dealing with storms, transcribing radio messages, wrestling the ocean, standing midnight watches, trying to fulfill promises we had made to help freedom prevail over those who seemed to us to be killing it.

We found that the country's success in that struggle gave our lives a special touch of meaning. And it aroused in us deathless gratitude for those who did not return, for those young and valuable bodies had to be laid on the hillsides of Oran or Okinawa, or reverently buried at sea.

When John wrote, "The victory that defeats the world is our faith" (I John 5:5 NEB), he was not writing about a Gold Medal Winner, a National League Championship, or a victory in war, but about one that surpasses all the other victories we know about.

It is the victory, he says, that overcomes both life and death. The victory of someone who has found something to believe in, someone to trust, something that outlives and outdies everything else we know.

It is living boldly, bravely, compassionately, honestly, without guarantees.

My favorite definition of faith has long been Kirsopp Lake's: "Faith is not belief in spite of evidence, but life in scorn of consequence."

Someone else says that faith is "hanging on five minutes longer."

Washington Gladden gave me something to remember permanently about the life of trust when he wrote:

And fierce though the fiends may fight, / And long though the angels hide, / I know that Truth and Right / Have the universe on their side.

I know only in part, faith says, but there is *something* I know, and I am ready to build my life around that.

We do not know much about the future except that there are only about fifteen years left in this millennium. We do know, though, something about our own moral and spiritual insides—that it is up to us to decide whether the future that is out there waiting is something that intimidates us, or rattles us, or makes us anxious and afraid, or whether Studdert-Kennedy's splendid spirit will enable us to grasp that future and shape it so that it conforms to some kind of holy purpose.

Some imagine God as the Man Upstairs, the celestial giant, whose power is unlimited and who pulls on all the strings and pushes all the buttons—part starkeeper and king, judge, ruler, super-architect, a boss.

But then Jesus comes, Good Friday comes, and we begin to discover a God who knows even more about suffering and helplessness than he does about sovereignty. He emerges out of the shadows of our prolix theology as Someone who cares.

Though we do not know all the answers about God or the reason life is arranged the way it is, we do know this: God cares about us and he cares about the world he has made.

God is *for* us no matter what.

Accept No Imitations

No matter that we are not all the things we think we would like to be.

No matter that we have stopped believing in ourselves. God believes in us. God is in our corner. He is the Good Samaritan who stops at the scene of the accident or the robbery. Never the *inflicter* of pain, God is the wounded healer instead.

In *Experiences of God* (Fortress Press, 1980), Jurgen Moltmann says that faith shares in God's protest by fighting against death in the midst of life. He says:

> Death is the evil power already existing in life's midst, not just at its end. Here is the economic death of the starving; there the political death of the oppressed. Here is the social death of the handicapped. There a noisy death through bombs. Here again, the silent death of petrified souls. The raising of Christ is proved by our courage to rise *against* death. It is only in our passion for life and in giving of ourselves for its liberation that we trust ourselves utterly to God's grace.

Another way to say this may be to say that God is in love with life, therefore in love with us.

If something angry inside of us lashes back at that sort of "nonsense" and says God has funny and illogical ways of showing such concern, then we must deal with two other issues. The first asks, What God are we talking about? Is the God against whom we may lodge such a complaint about the way the world is arranged *really* the God of the Bible, or is he some false deity of our own imagining? If we want to challenge God, and we should if we hope to grow up, we must make sure we know *what* God we are challenging.

The second issue is to be equally careful and specific about what we make the word *death* mean.

Moltmann puts us on notice that the death of the body is not the death to be most concerned about. God's "passion for life," to use his phrase, is life in all its magical constructions. It is the life of the soul, the life of the imagination, the life of wonder, of invention, of tasting, of seeing, of dreaming, and of daring.

Norman Cousins has said, "The tragedy is not that we die, but what dies within us while we live."

We are God's indestructible community of hope and witnesses to what God's power can do. God within us. God beside us. God preceding us.

"Why are you cast down, O my soul, / and why are you disquieted within me?" the psalmist prayed (Ps. 42:5*a*).

But his dejection was also matched by something else inside him that cried out its contradiction.

He remembers beautiful days when he marched with the multitudes to the temple, chanting the songs of faith. And his heart finds rest in this unyielding fragment of confidence. "By day the Lord commands his steadfast love; / and at night his song is with me" (Ps. 42:8*a*).

He could have added, "I remember beauty, and my father and mother, and fragrant mornings, and a million moments of childhood's splendor." He calls God his "rock." And his conclusion he addresses to his own heart: "Hope in God; for I shall again praise him" (Ps. 42:11a).

We are all jugglers, trying to keep all our pins in the air, trying to intersect with God who is not immobile like a mountain or tree, but who is action and who shows himself both through plain expressions of love, and in tragic contests between good and evil. His love shines, not as a steady light, but as a stuttering, sometimes uncertain illumination against the darkness.

The hope that radicalizes our hearts is ours both to keep and to give away. It still makes giants of men, just as it once changed a braided circle of thorns into the crown of a thirty-three-year-old carpenter.

> He whom a dream hath possessed knoweth no more of doubting,
> For mist and the blowing of winds and the mouthing of words he scorns.
> No sinuous speech and smooth he hears, but a knightly shouting,
> And never comes darkness down, yet he greeteth a million morns.
>
> He whom a dream hath possessed knoweth no more of roaming.
> All roads and the flowing of waves and the speediest flight he knows,
> But wherever his feet are set, his soul is forever homing,
> And going he comes, and coming he heareth a call and goes.

Raised Arms and Scoreboard Lights

He whom a dream hath possessed knoweth no more of sorrow.
At death and the dropping of leaves and the fading of sun he smiles,
For a dream remembers no past and takes no thought of a morrow,
And staunch amid seas of doom a dream sets the ultimate isles.

He whom a dream hath possessed treads the impalpable marches.
From the dust of the day's long road he leaps to a laughing star,
And the ruin of worlds that fall he views from eternal arches,
And rides God's battlefield in a flashing and golden car.
                                        Shaemas O'Sheel

The new, then, is never totally new; it is always preceded by a dream. And the kingdom is always preceded by hope. It is the womb in which tomorrow is conceived. When it is born and renamed today, it turns into a pair of coveralls, a decorated bicycle, a ham-and-cheese sandwich, and a stage band.

Nothing Dies That Is Remembered

Life is funny, isn't it? And death is funny, too. I wonder about these old people who want to live more and more, I can't understand it. It seems after 80 we should be reconciled to leave room for younger life and go off courteously, joyously. But nobody seems to agree with me. Everybody's miserable about dying. And I say nonsense. I don't mean that life is a pain to me. I enjoy every minute of it. But I realize I've shot my bolt and somebody should come along and take me away. . . .

So I think a great deal should be said for death. So let's be happy. We're all going to die. It's wonderful. Do you realize that? —Will Durant, quoted in the *Los Angeles Times*, June 1, 1980

Truman Douglas has called the church "man's rememberer," and we thank him for that.

Remembrance is a sacrament, a grace, an active power for living our way into the future.

Prisoners of war survive by remembrance, and so do nations.

The present can happen only once, and the psalmist is correct when he says of our human experience: "We last no longer than a dream. / We are like weeds that sprout in the morning, / that grow and burst into bloom, / then dry up and die in the evening" (Ps. 90:5-6 TEV).

But nothing dies that is remembered.

Time has flown so quickly we say
And history can't come back. All
That stays of 30,000 yesterdays
Are a few, faint foottracks 'cross
The heart. Mental tapes of days,
And ways we knew. Or, thank God, were known.

Nothing Dies That Is Remembered

The memory of heaven's perfect,
Even if not our own.

James W. Angell

Three friends died during the brief span of months this book has been in process—good friends whose legacy has been themselves. Ted's humility and freedom from pretension. John's twinkled grin and patience with my poor golf shots while his were always straight and long down the fairway. And Wes, whose surgeon hands were matched by an equal skill in poised courage. He lives on in me, too, giving new dimension to my soul.

Nothing dies that is remembered.

Robert Ardrey, in *African Genesis* (Atheneum, 1961), has something eloquent to say about the ingredients of true humanness and about remembering:

> Time and death and the space between the stars remain of the substance of evolution and of all that we are. They rest unseen in a gesture of farewell, in a handshake or kiss, or a child's goodnight. We read a book, or think of friends, or remember our grandmother's little grey house where a trumpet vine softened the kitchen window. We go to bed, or build a pyramid, or accomplish a peak in Darien and stand hushed by the view of an unknown sea. We fear. We regret. We learn or love. It is all of a piece, and the moment of our consciousness is the moment of all things.

In this book we have been involved in trying to make value judgments about religion. And if we seem to have lost our way spiritually, lost a sense of history—which may explain why we have become so vulnerable to frauds and lies—the way back to health may be partly through remembrance.

In religion, as with the rest of the human agenda, the quality of the future will be related to the quality of our remembering.

Jesus asks us to remember who we are. It was only after the prodigal son had come "to himself" that the scales were tipped to the side of hope.

We are also to remember those in trouble—the poor, the underloved and overlooked, the desolate and dying.

And we must remember all those promises! Not the ones we are obligated to keep, but the ones that keep us, that mold us into vessels of hope and walking computers of memory.

There's a famous old Scotch story by Ian Maclaren entitled *Beside the Bonnie Brier Bush* about a beloved doctor who practiced medicine in a village known as Drumtochty. For more than fifty years he loved the people, listening to them—and to their chests—making trips over washboard roads in the middle of the night to anxious bedsides, delivering their children, uttering final words of comfort, "he's at peace now."

Then this beautiful old man died. The day of his funeral service in the kirk, a heavy snow fell, making travel over the narrow Scottish trails and roads nearly impossible. This did not stop the people from coming though. As everyone in the village plodded through tall white drifts, several elders of the church who had arrived early were warming themselves around a big

Nothing Dies That Is Remembered

stove, observing the arrival of the mourners. One turned to the other and said: "Well, here they come, and every one of them has his own reason."

That is remembering. Remembering helps us understand our selfhood. Some remembering makes us sad. Some qualifies us to know the difference between right and wrong. Some tells us where we have been, and that helps us create a map showing us where we may wish to go.

Matthew Panko, a Czech immigrant, in an article entitled "Thanks Mom, Thanks Pop," wrote: "It was a good childhood. We were poor, but I wish I had such wealth now."

A similar note is sounded by Paul: "Remember Jesus Christ, risen from the dead, descended from David, as preached in my gospel" (II Tim. 2:8).

And out of a rich affection for the little company of disciples he had grown to love in Philippi, Paul wrote, his hand inching across the paper as he sat near the window of a shadowed prison cell, "I thank my God in all my remembrance of you" (Phil. 1:3).

The remembering we do in worship is more than recall. It is remembering with a purpose:

We remember in order to follow.
We remember in order to do.
We remember in order to be.

For our wedding anniversary, Virginia and I received, as a surprise benediction, a tape from our daughter, Ann, who lives in Atlanta, Georgia. We

Accept No Imitations

saved it to play on the actual day of the anniversary, and settled down to listen to it that evening after dinner at a nearby restaurant.

We expected it to be a message of congratulations, good wishes from our beloved first-born. Imagine our amazement when the message turned out to be very different. It was a recording made thirteen years before of a family Christmas. The year was 1969. And because we were all together that year, except for Ann, we had turned on a recorder on Christmas Eve, and again Christmas morning, so that her family would be able to enjoy all that took place. Little did we imagine that before another Christmas one of our children, our lovely twenty-one-year-old Susan, would be taken by death in an automobile accident. And the remarkable thing about the tape, which we had totally forgotten about, was that it contained her voice and violin rendition of "O Holy Night," plus the voices and laughter and joke-making of all of us. It is the only living sound of her voice we have!

Nothing dies that is remembered!

Death, though, is part of life. And life could not be the fantastic, fragile, suffering mystery it is without death. Death often seems like the enemy that always manages to have the final word but it is probably more friend than adversary. What greater gift can we imagine from God at this point than a grand new beginning, free of pain, alive with the prospect of new becomings, even joyful reunions.

Nothing Dies That Is Remembered

We sometimes wish we had the power to stop the hands of the clock, bottle up moonbeams, freeze-frame the present, hold the deep changes that come to us permanently at bay.

Jesse Stuart wrote:

> If only I could command the sun to stop where it was in the sky and hold all the white mists where they were in the air. If I could keep the pasture daisies as white, and the wild roses as pink as they were now. If I could keep the sawbriers in clusters with their red-tinted leaves. If I could make this pasture and time stand still I'd do it.

But life is the Columbia River, not Fort Knox.

Someone has said history might be likened to a motion picture which could be run backward through a projector as well as forward; it makes equal nonsense either way. But against such verdicts of meaninglessness stands a gospel, a promise, and a possibility.

And between patternless absurdities and daring hope, we must make a choice, and do.

Those who plunge into the waters become life's salt, leaven, and light. Their presence is *already making a difference* in the outcome of things, for hope is not empty dreaming. When we hope, the spiritual chemistry of the world is already being affected.

If faith is courage that has said its prayers, hope is faith that has jumped, pulled the rip cord, and shouted, "Geronimo!"

It is a raindrop which, when sunlight glances off it,

Accept No Imitations

reflects three strong but complementary colors: past, present, and future.

Vladimir Rojansky taught physics at Harvey Mudd College in Claremont, California. As a young man he was part of a White Russian army that retreated four thousand miles across Siberia on horseback until it stood backed against the sea.

When the defeated force was ultimately disbanded, "Ro" discovered a way to come to the United States to attend a college and start life over. His immigration papers, though, lacked a necessary identifying photograph, and he was at the point of missing out on what seemed to him the greatest opportunity of his life. But the little seacoast village where he was mustered out had no place to get a picture taken in time to make the sailing.

After his papers had been examined and rejected by one official at the immigration office, the disappointed ex-soldier went for a walk through the half-deserted streets of the town.

Wandering past the office a second time, he looked through the window and noticed another clerk checking the papers of ex-soldiers. So he tried that line, getting a similar result.

Later, a third.

"Sorry, you must have a picture."

It was dark, time for the office to close, when Vladimir Rojansky made a fourth and final try at the immigration office.

Nothing Dies That Is Remembered

On this attempt, yet another clerk was in the process of explaining to him why his papers were not complete when the clerk looked up from the much-handled documents, as if struggling to remember something, and said, "Rojansky.... Did you ever know anyone who worked on the Trans-Siberian railroad named Rojansky? Once, after I had been wounded in the fighting, I was being transported, along with other wounded soldiers, in a box car. It was night, and cold. The box car was in poor condition and the wind blew through a big hole in one side. We were freezing as we pulled into some little place and stopped. A man who worked on the railroad came along about then and patched the hole so that we could be warmer. His name—I'm sure of it—was Rojansky."

"That was my father," said Ro, clutching hope in his half-despondent, war-weary hands.

He was on the ship as it sailed to America!

From out of its fetal past, hope is borne across the years to us. Often it comes on the wings of solemn beauty—and with strange extra-worldly scar-ridden authority—the authority of weakness. Yet nothing is its match.

So we go on living by faith—walking by faith rather than by sight, knowing life is always a loan, not an outright transfer of title. In the presence of death we see life more clearly, treasure it more dearly, use it with an ever-renewed sense of awe.

Accept No Imitations

So don't take any wooden emeralds. But if anyone offers you real ones, don't turn them down. They are loaded with ancient sunlight, just as the days of your own years are crowded with splendor someone else may someday recall.